THE CHILDREN'S STEP-BY-STEP COOK BOOK

BY
ANGELA WILKES

TED SMART

A DORLING KINDERSLEY BOOK

For Sam, Rose, and Roger

Art Editor Jane Bull
Photography Dave King
Home Economist Jane Suthering

Editor Anna Kunst
Managing Art Editor Jacquie Gulliver
Managing Editor Susan Peach

Production Shelagh Gibson
DTP Designer James W Hunter

First published in Great Britain in 1994
by Dorling Kindersley Limited,
A Penguin Company,
80 Strand, London, WC2R ORL

14 16 18 20 19 17 15 13

This edition produced for The Book People Ltd,
Hall Wood Avenue, Haydock, St Helens WA11 9UL

A CIP catalogue record for this book is available from the British Library.

ISBN 0-7513-5121-0

Reproduced by Bright Arts in Hong Kong
Printed and bound in China by Toppan Printing Co., Ltd.

CONTENTS

COOKING FOR BEGINNERS **6**

KITCHEN RULES **8**

COOK'S TOOLS **10**

12

SNACKS

SNACKS ON STICKS **14**

SANDWICH FILLINGS **16**

FINGER BITES **18**

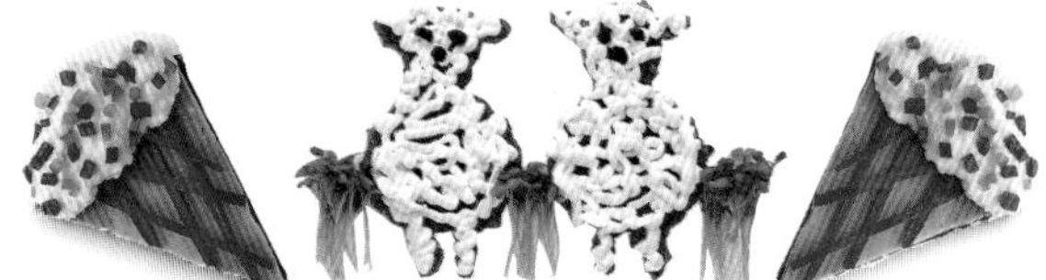

MEALS IN ROLLS **20**

ICE LOLLIES **22**

POPCORN **23**

MILKSHAKES 24

26 EGGS AND CHEESE

SIMPLE EGGS 28

EGGS IN POTS 29

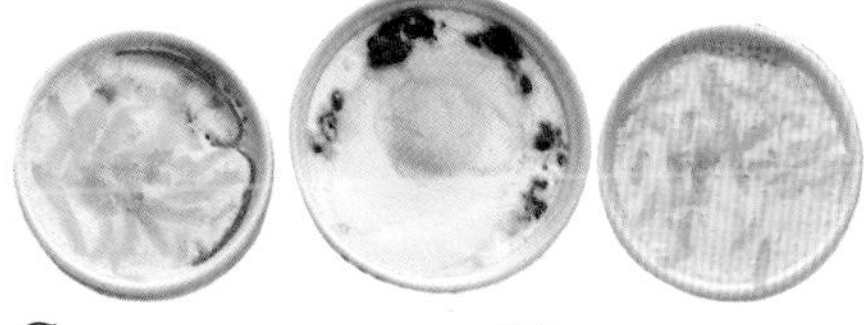

SCRAMBLED EGGS 30

FRENCH TOAST AND CINNAMON TOAST 32

TOASTY TREATS 34

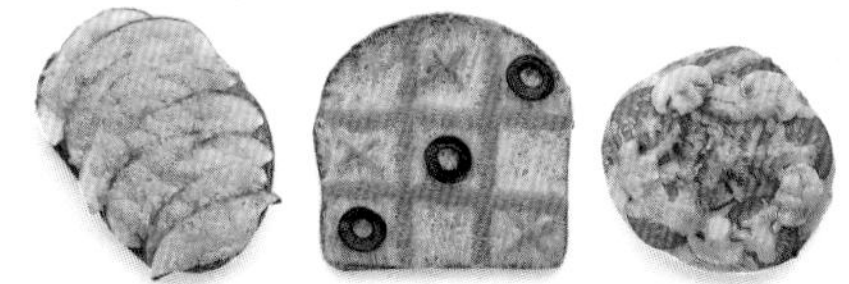

QUICHES AND TARTS 36

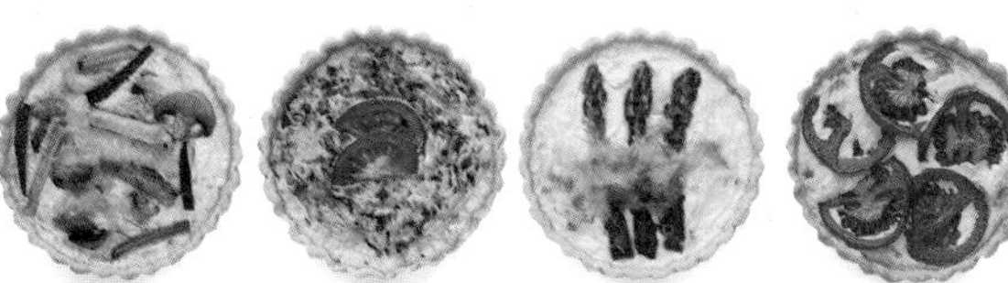

40 PASTA, RICE, AND PIZZA

CREAMY SPAGHETTI 42

PASTA SAUCES 44

VEGETABLES AND RICE 46

CHINESE FRIED RICE 48

PIZZA FEAST 50

52

VEGETABLES

COOKING VEGETABLES 54

SALAD TIME 56

JACKET POTATOES 58

CHEESE AND POTATO BAKE 60

COWBOY BEAN BAKE 62

64

MEAT AND FISH

HAMBURGER FEAST 66

KEBABS 68

SPICY CHICKEN 70

BEEF CASSEROLE 72

FISHERMAN'S PIE 74

76

BISCUITS, BREAD, AND CAKES

GINGERBREAD FOLK 78

ICING BISCUITS 80

CHOCOLATE CHIP COOKIES 82

BAKING BREAD 84

FUNNY ROLLS 86

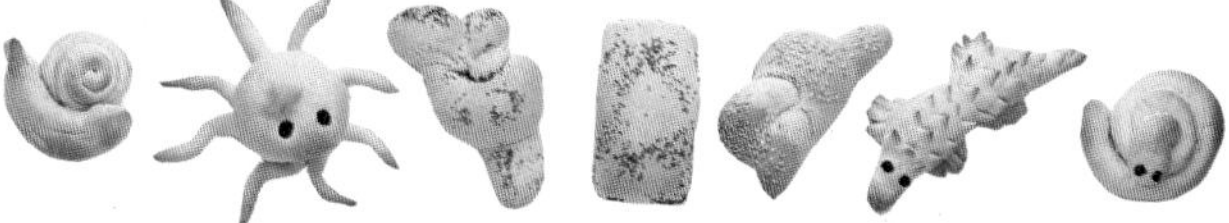

LITTLE CAKES 88
ICING LITTLE CAKES 90

ICED SPONGE CAKE 92
CAKE DECORATING 94

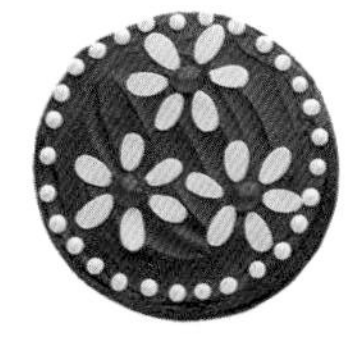

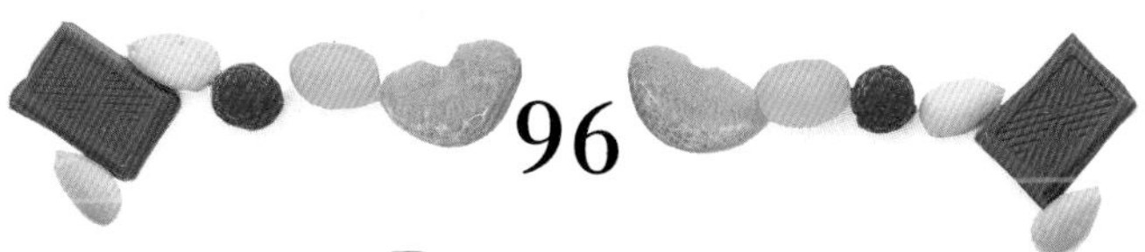

96

PUDDINGS AND TREATS

ICE-CREAM SAUCES 98

CHOCOLATE TREATS 100

BISCUIT CAKE 102

FRUIT FRISBEES 104

FRUIT IN THE OVEN 106

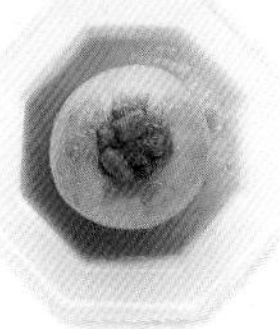

FRUIT BASKETS 108

APPLE PIE AND CUSTARD 110
DECORATING THE PIE 112

PANCAKE TIME 114

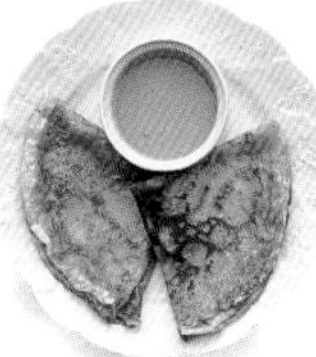

PICNIC TIME 116

PARTY TIME 118

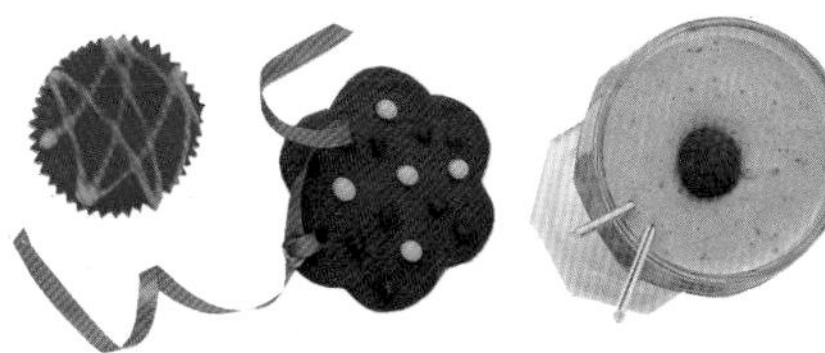

MENU PLANNER 120

PICTURE GLOSSARY 121

INDEX 127

COOKING FOR BEGINNERS

The CHILDREN'S STEP-BY-STEP COOKBOOK is full of easy-to-follow recipes for things that are fun to make and scrumptious to eat. From boiling an egg to creating the perfect apple pie, all the basic cooking skills are covered. You can learn how to make your own bread, whip up meringues, and make delicious sauces, and there are lots of suggestions on how to vary the recipes. There is also useful information about ingredients and a complete picture glossary.

THE CHAPTER OPENERS

The recipe part of the book is divided into seven chapters, such as "Vegetables". Each chapter starts with simple recipes and progresses to more advanced ones. At the beginning of the chapter there is a double-page information spread on ingredients like this one.

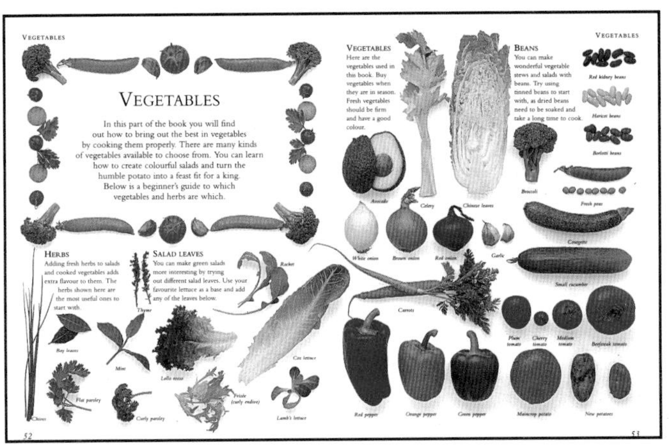

VEGETABLES

VEGETABLES

In this part of the book you will find out how to bring out the best in vegetables by cooking them properly. There are many kinds of vegetables available to choose from. You can learn how to create colourful salads and turn the humble potato into a feast fit for a king. Below is a beginner's guide to which vegetables and herbs are which.

HERBS
Adding fresh herbs to salads and cooked vegetables adds extra flavour to them. The herbs shown here are the most useful ones to start with.

SALAD LEAVES
You can make green salads more interesting by trying out different salad leaves. Use your favourite lettuce as a base and add any of the leaves below.

VEGETABLES
Here are the vegetables used in this book. Buy vegetables when they are in season. Fresh vegetables should be firm and have a good colour.

BEANS
You can make wonderful vegetable stews and salads with beans. Try using tinned beans to start with, as dried beans need to be soaked and take a long time to cook.

THE PICTURE GLOSSARY

The picture glossary on pages 121-126 explains all the most common cookery terms. Words that appear in the glossary are shown in italic type, like this: *simmer*. Look in the glossary for step-by-step picture guides to particular cookery techniques, such as creaming.

THE RECIPES

The ingredients
All the ingredients you need for each recipe are shown, so that you can check you have the right amounts.

The quantities
Each recipe tells you how many servings the ingredients make. Generally, each recipe serves four people.

Cook's tools
These illustrated checklists show you all the utensils you need to have ready before you start cooking.

PUDDINGS AND TREATS

CHOCOLATE TREATS

CHOCOLATE TREATS

Try these delicious nibbles – mini-florentines and chocolate-dipped fruit. You will need to allow at least one hour for the chocolate to set when making them. A 115 g (4 oz) bar of chocolate will make eight mini-florentines.

COOK'S TOOLS

Chopping board • Plate • Circle of non-stick silicone paper • Sharp knife Saucepan • 2 teaspoons • 2 bowls

You will need (for 4 servings)

Good quality white chocolate
Mixed nuts
Glacé cherries
White grapes
Sultanas or raisins
Strawberries
Good quality milk chocolate
Dried apricots
Tangerine segments

Mini-florentines

1 Break the chocolate up into the two bowls. Put the white chocolate in one bowl and the milk chocolate in the other.

2 Heat water in a saucepan and stand each bowl in it in turn over a low heat. Stir the chocolate until it has melted.

3 Put the silicone paper on the plate and drop teaspoons of brown and white melted chocolate on to it.

4 Chop the cherries and dried apricots, then arrange the fruit and nuts on the chocolate and put it in a cool place to set.

Chocolate dips

1 Dip strawberries, grapes, and tangerine segments halfway into the melted chocolate, then lay them on the silicone paper.

2 Put the treats in a cool place for one to two hours until the chocolate has set hard. Then peel them gently off the paper.

Tasty treats

Arrange the mini-florentines and chocolate-dipped fruits in a pretty pattern on a plate. Store the treats in a cool place, but not in the fridge.

Mini-florentine
Chocolate-dipped tangerine segment
Chocolate-dipped strawberry
Chocolate-dipped grape

100 101

Step-by-step photos
Step-by-step photographs and easy-to-follow instructions show you what to do at each stage of every recipe.

The oven glove symbol
The oven glove symbol means that you have to do something that could be dangerous (such as using the oven, or the blender) and you should ask an adult to help you.

The finishing touches
These pictures show you how to garnish or decorate the things you have made and ways of serving them.

KITCHEN RULES

Cooking is fun, but hot cookers and sharp knives can also make it dangerous, so it is very important to learn some basic safety rules. They are illustrated here to make it easier to remember them. Read the rules carefully and follow them whenever you are cooking.

Be careful!

Never cook anything unless there is an adult there to help you. This oven glove symbol is a safety warning. Whenever you see the symbol next to a picture, it means you should ask an adult for help. Every time you chop something with a sharp knife, use the oven, or just need advice, ask your adult friend to help you.

Weighing and measuring

Each recipe gives both metric and imperial measurements. It is important to keep to one set of measurements or the other, as it is not possible to convert one to the other exactly. A "spoonful" in this book means a level spoonful.

Using the cooker

Always ask an adult to turn the oven on for you. Some ovens should be switched on to the temperature given in the recipe before you start cooking, so that they have heated up when you need to use them. Don't open the oven door while things are cooking. Follow the cooking times given in the recipe. And don't forget to turn the oven off when you have finished cooking!

Oven temperatures

Temperatures on electric ovens are normally shown in either Celsius (°C) or Fahrenheit (°F). In Celsius, 100° is boiling point, whereas in Fahrenheit 100° is more or less the temperature of the human body. On gas ovens, the temperature is measured in gas marks, from 1-9.

Conversion chart

Gas Mark	°F	°C
1	275	140
2	300	150
3	325	170
4	350	180
5	375	190
6	400	200
7	425	220
8	450	230
9	475	240

1 Before you start cooking, wash your hands and put on an apron. You may need to roll up your sleeves too.

5 When you are cooking on top of the cooker, turn the saucepan handles to the side, so you do not knock them.

9 Always wear oven gloves when picking up anything hot, or when putting things into or taking them out of the oven.

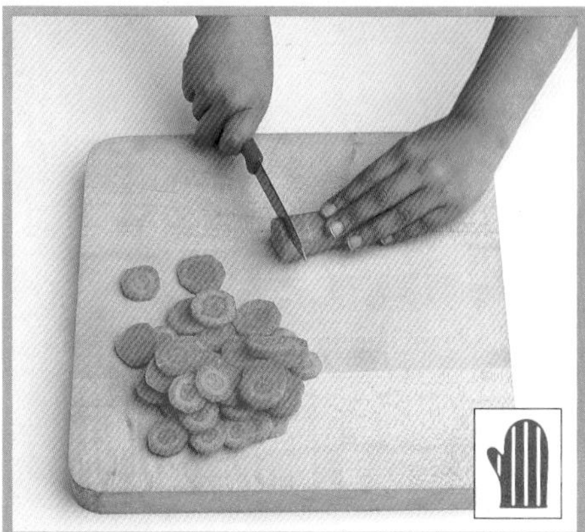

2 Collect all the ingredients together. Weigh the dry ingredients and measure the liquid ones in a measuring jug.

3 Check the recipe as you do this, to make sure that you have everything you need and know exactly what to do.

4 Be very careful with sharp knives. Hold them with the blade pointing downwards and always use a chopping board.

6 When you are stirring food in a pan, use a wooden spoon and hold the pan firmly by the handle.

7 Whenever you find it difficult to do something or have to handle hot things, ask an adult to help you.

8 Have a space ready for hot things. Put them on a mat or a wooden board, not straight on to a table or work surface.

10 Always make sure your hands are dry before you plug in or disconnect an electric gadget, such as a blender.

11 Keep a cloth nearby so that you can wipe up any spills. Clean up anything that spills on the floor immediately.

12 Wash up as you go along. When you have finished cooking, put everything away and clean up any mess.

COOK'S TOOLS

Here are all the utensils you will need to follow the recipes in this book. You will also need some kitchen scales, so that you can weigh the ingredients. You will find a checklist of the cook's tools that you need at the beginning of each recipe.

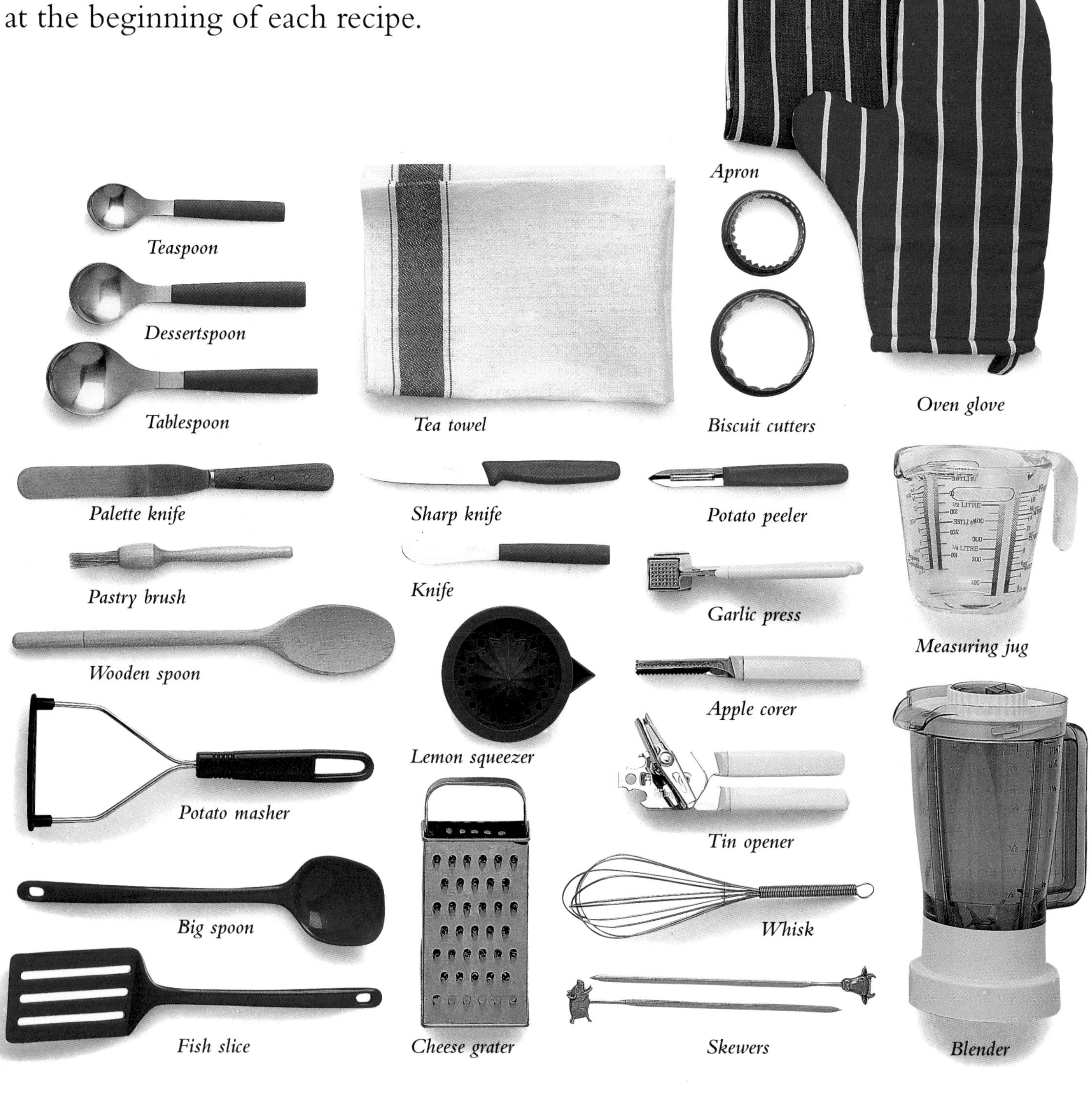

Apron

Teaspoon

Dessertspoon

Tablespoon

Tea towel

Biscuit cutters

Oven glove

Palette knife

Sharp knife

Potato peeler

Measuring jug

Pastry brush

Knife

Garlic press

Wooden spoon

Lemon squeezer

Apple corer

Potato masher

Tin opener

Big spoon

Whisk

Fish slice

Cheese grater

Skewers

Blender

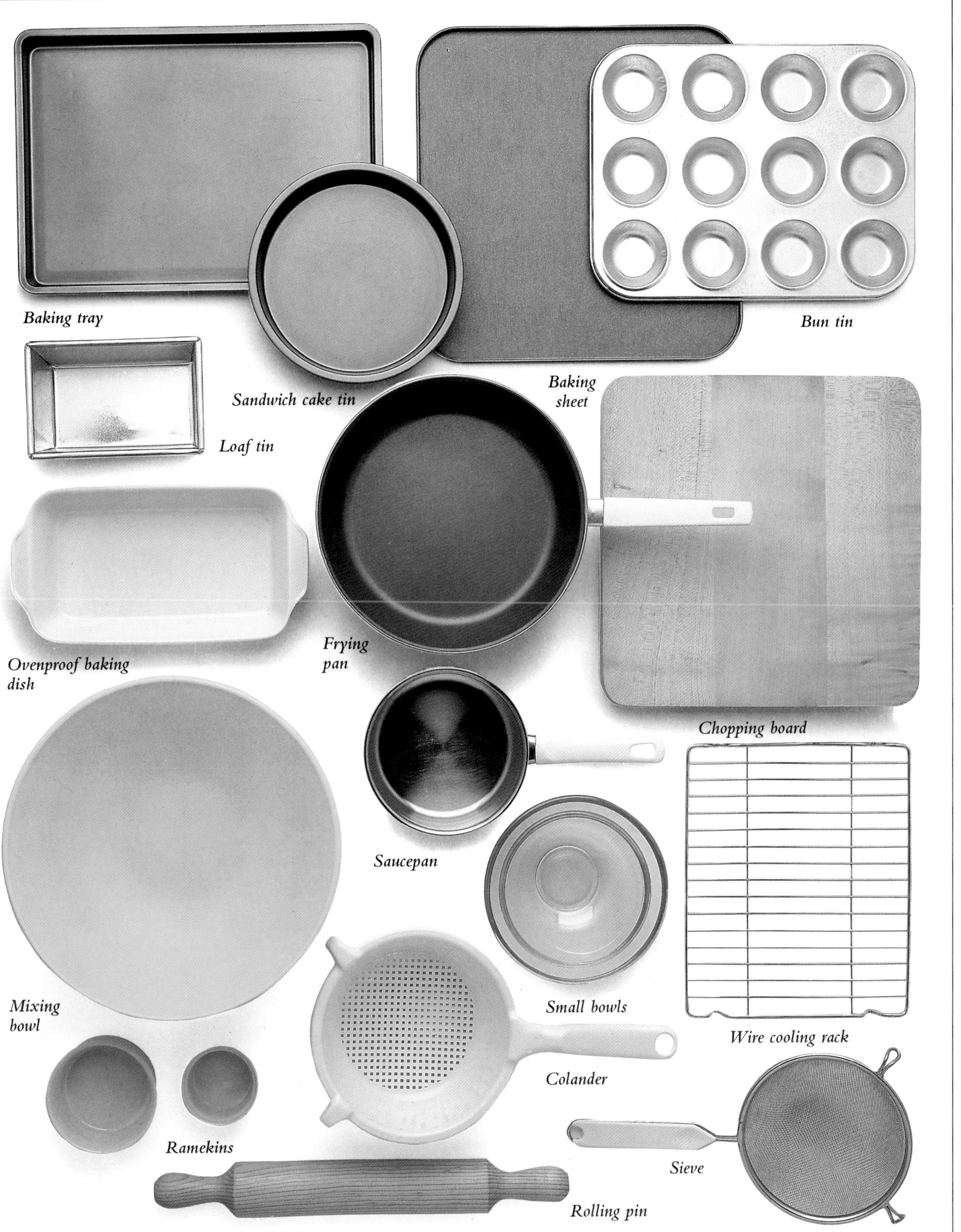
Baking tray
Bun tin
Sandwich cake tin
Baking sheet
Loaf tin
Ovenproof baking dish
Frying pan
Chopping board
Saucepan
Mixing bowl
Small bowls
Wire cooling rack
Colander
Ramekins
Sieve
Rolling pin

SNACKS

This book starts with snacks because they are quick, easy, and fun to prepare. A snack can be anything that fills those empty moments between main meals. It might be a creamy milkshake, popcorn, or a roll filled with some of your favourite things. Bread features in many snacks and so do cold meats. Here you can find out a bit more about them.

BREAD

There are many different types of breads. Try rye bread as well as white and brown bread made from wheat flour. Use sliced bread for sandwiches, stuff flat breads with salad, and look for unusual rolls from different countries.

English muffin *Mini-pitta bread*

Wholemeal mini-pitta bread

Sliced white bread *Dark rye bread* *Sliced wholemeal bread*

Italian white roll

COLD MEATS

These are mainly different kinds of cooked ham and sausage available at the delicatessen counter of supermarkets. Look for smoked and unsmoked ham and try out different kinds of spicy sausage.

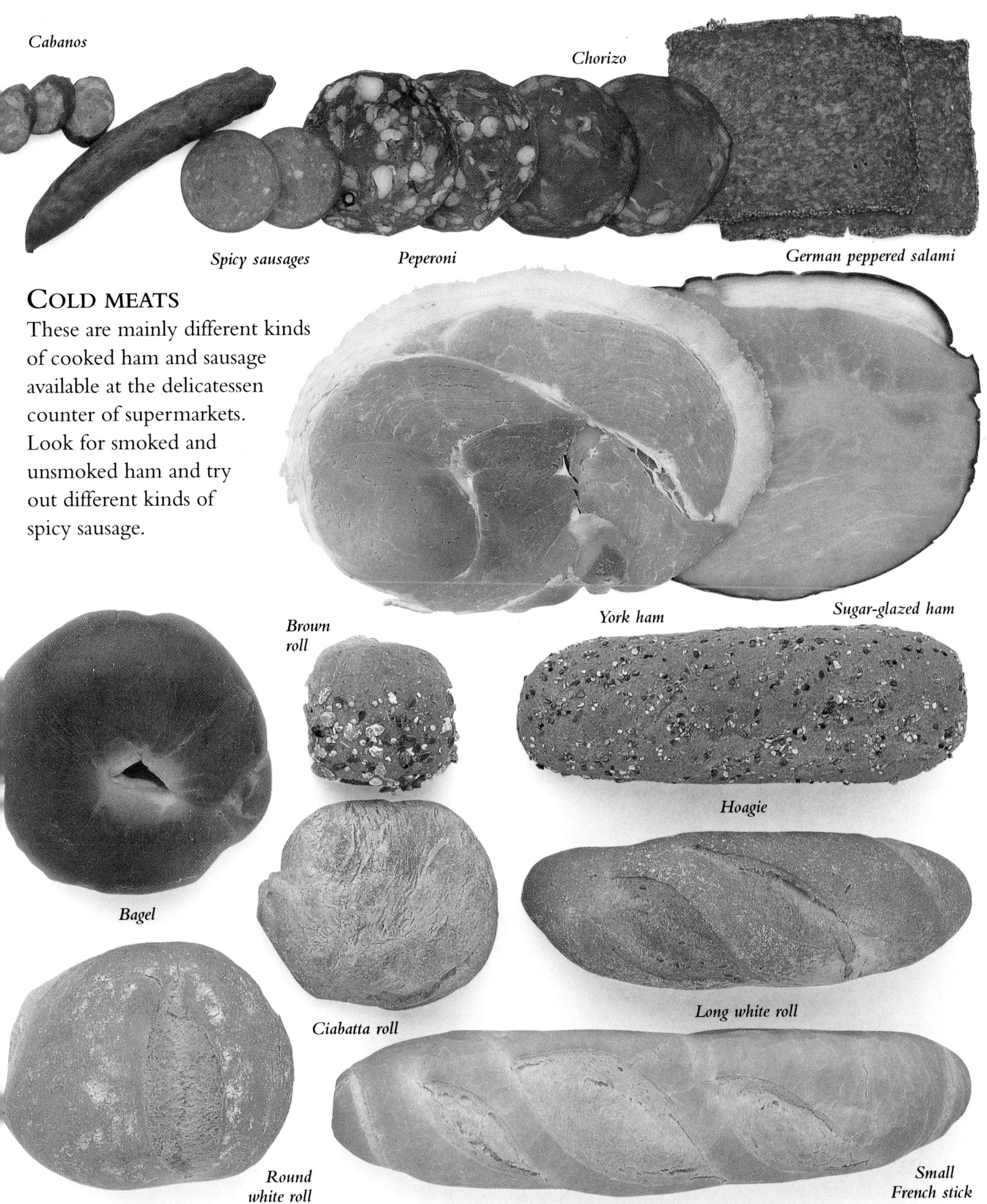

SNACKS ON STICKS

You can make simple kebabs with whatever you have at home. Try creating fruity ones, cheesy ones, or mixing sweet things with savoury things. Choose contrasting colours, and mix soft things with crunchy things. Here are some to try.

COOK'S TOOLS

Sharp knife • Potato peeler
Chopping board • Wooden skewers

You will need

(for 5 kebabs)

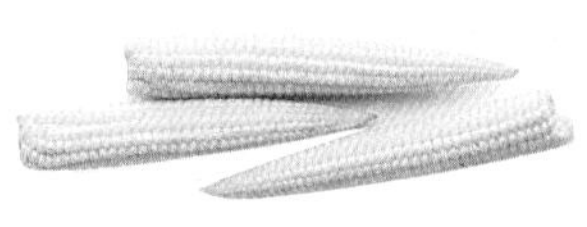

Baby sweetcorn

A green pepper

A carrot

Tinned mandarin oranges

Small tomatoes

Strawberries

A hard cheese

Salami

Pineapple cubes

A small bunch of grapes

Mozzarella cheese

Stuffed olives

Baby mushrooms

A peach

Small, cooked beetroots

Mangetout peas

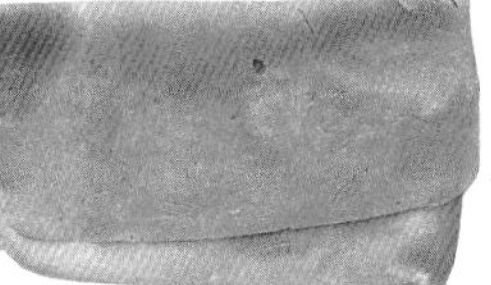

Sliced ham

Cooked Frankfurter sausages

What to do

1 Cut the cheese and sausages into chunks. Cut cubes of green pepper. Cut the carrot in half and peel it into long strips.

2 Decide which things you want to go together and start threading them on to a wooden skewer, one at a time.

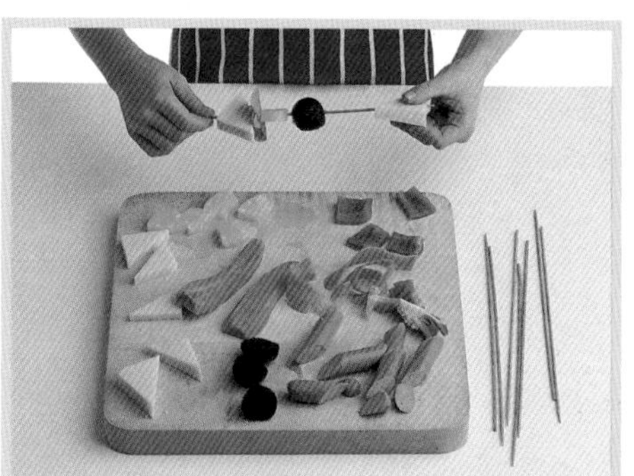

3 Carry on threading things on to the skewer until it is full, with just enough room at each end to hold it.

Rainbow kebabs

The finished kebabs are a good picnic or party treat. Slide everything off the skewer on to a plate with a fork. If not eaten at once, store in the fridge.

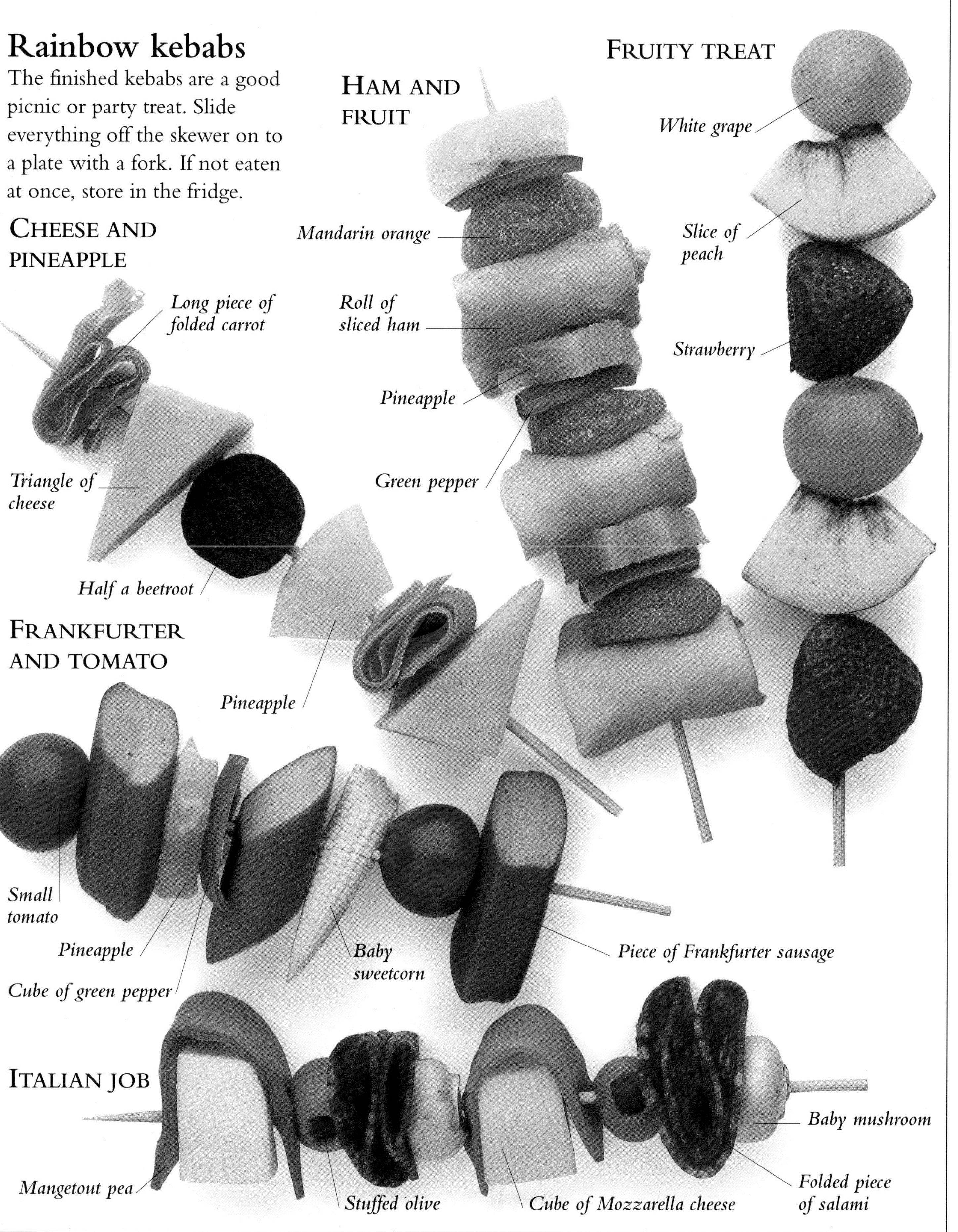

SANDWICH FILLINGS

Sandwiches and filled rolls are perfect snack food. On the next four pages you will find some ideas on how to use fillings in a variety of rolls and open sandwiches. It is best to store them in the fridge and eat within 24 hours.

COOK'S TOOLS

Chopping board • Small saucepan
Sharp knife • Fork
Cheese grater • Bowls

You will need (for 6 servings)

For avocado filling

1 avocado

1 finely chopped tomato

2 tablespoons fromage frais or soured cream

For any of the fillings

A pinch of salt

A pinch of pepper

For tuna filling

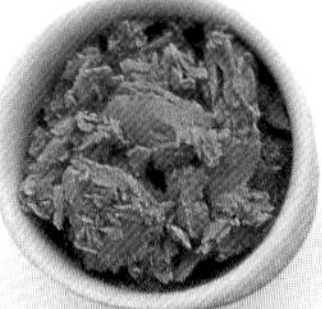

1 small tin of tuna

2 tablespoons mayonnaise

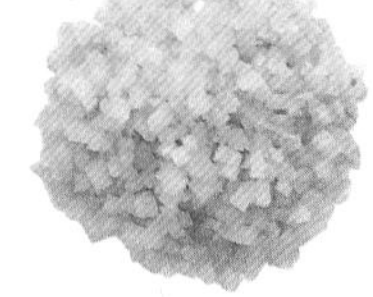

1 finely chopped stick of celery

1 finely chopped spring onion

For ham and chicken filling

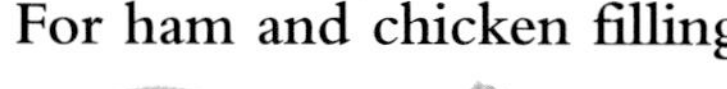

3 tablespoons fromage frais

55 g (2 oz) diced ham

1 diced, cooked chicken breast

1 tablespoon chopped parsley

For carrot and cheese filling

115 g (4 oz) grated carrot

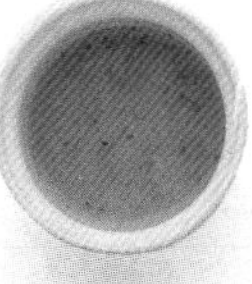

1 tablespoon salad dressing (see page 56)

115 g (4 oz) grated cheese

1 grated apple

For egg filling

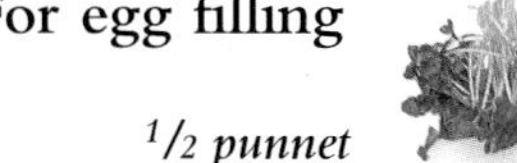

1/2 punnet mustard and cress

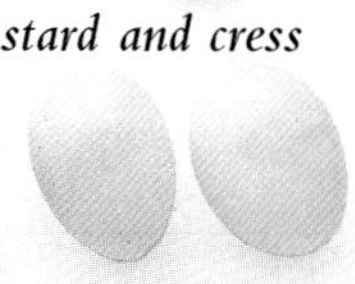

1 tablespoon mayonnaise

2 hard-boiled eggs

For creamy cheese filling

1/4 diced red pepper

115 g (4 oz) cream cheese

30 g (1 oz) chopped cucumber

CARROT AND CHEESE

TUNA

CREAMY CHEESE

Carrot and cheese

Put the *grated* cheese, carrot, and apple in a bowl. Add the salad dressing, salt, and pepper and mix everything together.

Tuna

Put the finely *chopped* spring onion and celery in a bowl with the drained tuna, mayonnaise, salt, and pepper and stir well.

Creamy cheese

Beat the cream cheese in a bowl with a fork until smooth, then mix in the red pepper, cucumber, salt, and pepper.

Ham and chicken

Beat the fromage frais in a bowl until it is smooth, then stir in the ham, chicken, parsley, salt, and pepper.

Egg mayonnaise

Boil the eggs in the saucepan (see page 28), then mash them in a bowl. Add the mustard and cress, mayonnaise, salt, and pepper.

Avocado

Cut the avocado in half and take out the stone. Scoop the flesh into a bowl and mash it, then stir in the tomato and fromage frais.

HAM AND CHICKEN

EGG MAYONNAISE

AVOCADO

FINGER BITES

When you want something special for tea or a party, have fun creating these tiny sandwiches, where everything is arranged on top of firm bread or toast. Try the ideas shown here, or invent some of your own. Eat immediately.

COOK'S TOOLS

Biscuit cutters • Teaspoon • Knife
Sharp knife • Chopping board

You will need

(for 4 servings)

Sliced firm bread, such as rye bread

Stuffed olives

Cherry tomatoes

Shredded lettuce

Tuna filling *(see pages 16-17)*

Round rolls or muffins

Small, long brown rolls

Currants

Tinned red kidney beans

Strips of pepper

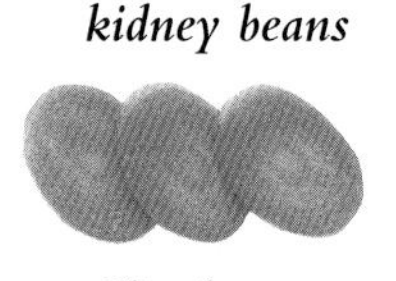

Sliced carrots

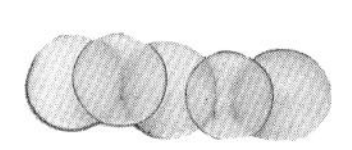

Sliced radishes

Cream cheese

Creamy scrambled egg *(see pages 30-31)*

Sliced cheese and ham

Sliced cucumber

Cress

Funny faces

1 Take a muffin or bread roll and cut it in half. You can use each half to make a funny face sandwich.

2 Cut out a circle of sliced cheese and lay it on the roll. Add a mouth cut out of cheese and two slices of cucumber.

3 Use lettuce for eyebrows and two halves of tomato for eyes. Stick a kidney bean to the face with cream cheese for a nose.

Tutti frutti ice-cream

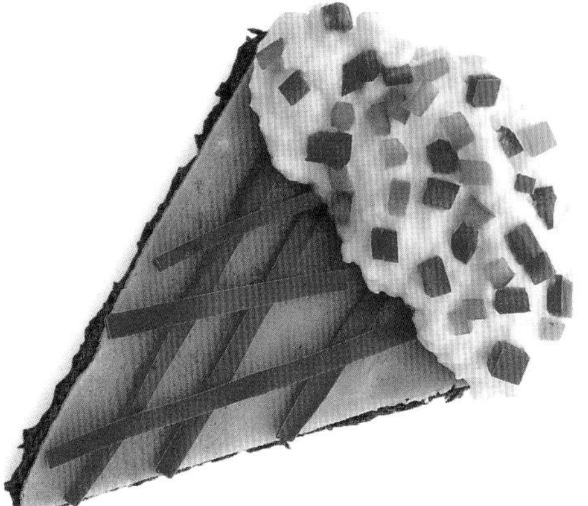

1 Take a slice of bread and cut the ends off diagonally so that it takes the shape of an ice-cream cone, as shown above.

2 Cut out a triangle of ham for the cone and lay it on the bread. Spoon scrambled egg above it to look like ice-cream.

3 Lay strips of red pepper in a criss-cross pattern on the cone and sprinkle finely *diced* peppers on the scrambled egg.

Woolly sheep

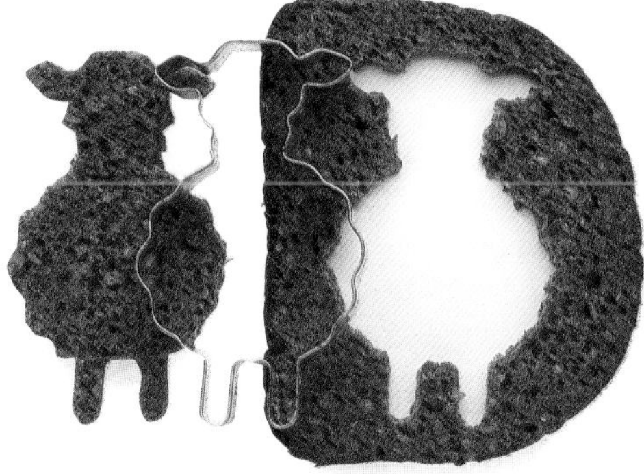
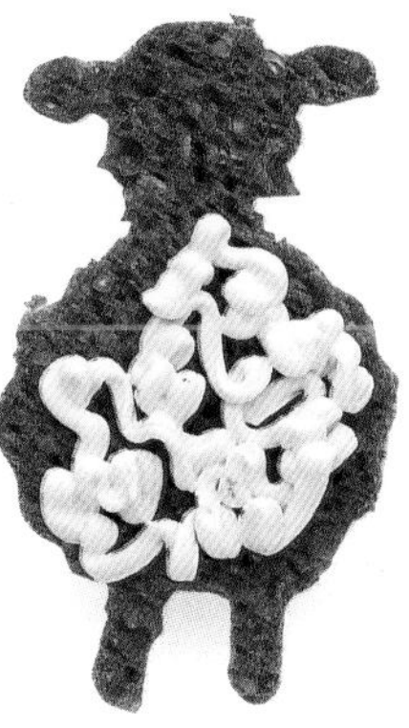

1 Use a biscuit cutter to cut sheep out of slices of brown bread. Or use the cutters you have to cut out other animals.

2 Spread cream cheese over the sheep. If the cheese is in a tube, squeeze it out in wiggly lines to look like wool.

3 Add currants to make eyes and noses, and snip off tiny bunches of cress to make green grass for munching.

Freddy flounder

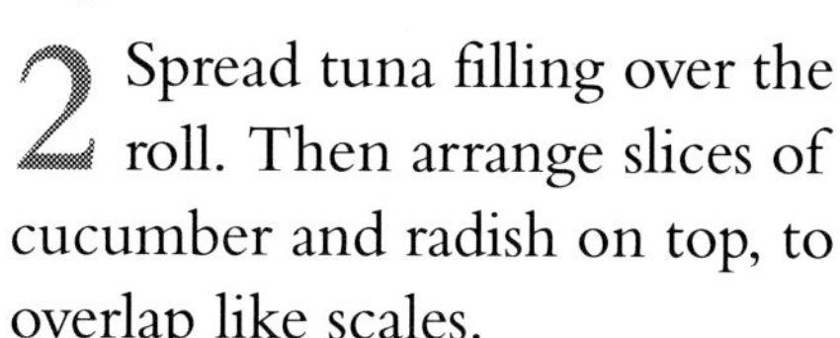

1 Take a long roll and slice off one end. Then cut out two triangles – one at the top and one at the bottom of the roll.

2 Spread tuna filling over the roll. Then arrange slices of cucumber and radish on top, to overlap like scales.

3 Add triangles of sliced carrot for fins and half an olive for an eye, and make a mouth out of squares of red pepper.

MEALS IN ROLLS

Filled rolls don't only make good snacks. You can eat them for lunch or tea and at picnics and parties. Try using different sorts of bread and mixing the fillings you have made with crunchy salad vegetables and ham, cheese, or sausage. Eat within 24 hours.

COOK'S TOOLS

Chopping board
Sharp knife • Spoon

You will need (for 5 rolls)

Different sorts of rolls

White roll

Italian round roll

Small pitta breads

Sliced salami

Small lettuce leaves

Strips of bacon or smoked ham

Tomatoes

Brown roll with seeds on top

Sliced cheese

Sliced ham

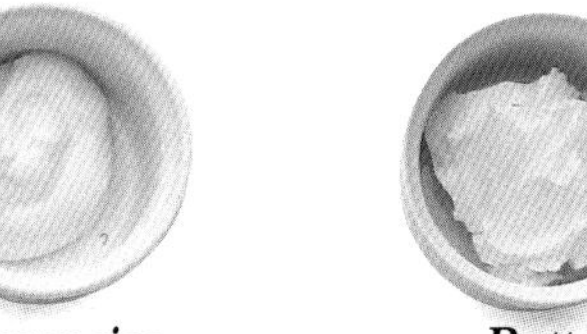

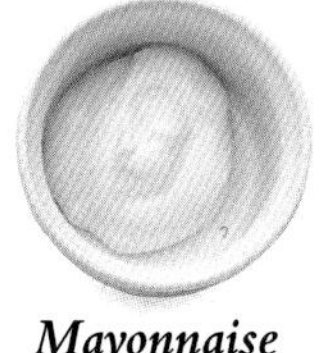

Mayonnaise

Butter

Tuna filling (see pages 16-17)

Egg mayonnaise (see pages 16-17)

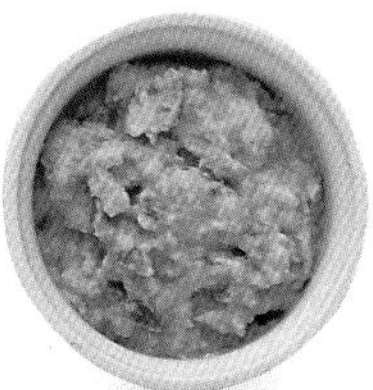

Avocado filling (see pages 16-17)

Greek salad (see pages 56-57)

What to do

1 Carefully cut along each roll lengthways, then open the roll and spread both halves with a little butter or mayonnaise.

2 Spoon filling on to one half of the roll (or into the bread if using pitta bread). Spread the filling out evenly over the roll.

3 Arrange the other ingredients on top. These slices of salami are folded in half, then in half again to make a butterfly shape.

MINI-PITTAS
Wholemeal pitta bread
Greek salad
Avocado filling
Grilled bacon or smoked ham
White pitta bread
ROUND ROLL
Tuna filling
Lettuce
Sliced tomato
Round roll
TORPEDO
Lettuce
Sliced cheese
Sliced tomato
Sliced ham
GOLDEN ROLL
Egg mayonnaise
Folded salami

ICE LOLLIES

What better snack on a hot day than an ice lolly? Here you can find out how to make your own lollies from fruit juice and fruit yogurt. The quantities shown will make about three of each sort. They will take about two hours to freeze.

You will need (for 6 lollies)

For fruity yogurt lolly

75 ml (2 1/2 fl oz) blackcurrant syrup

150 ml (5 fl oz) strawberry yogurt

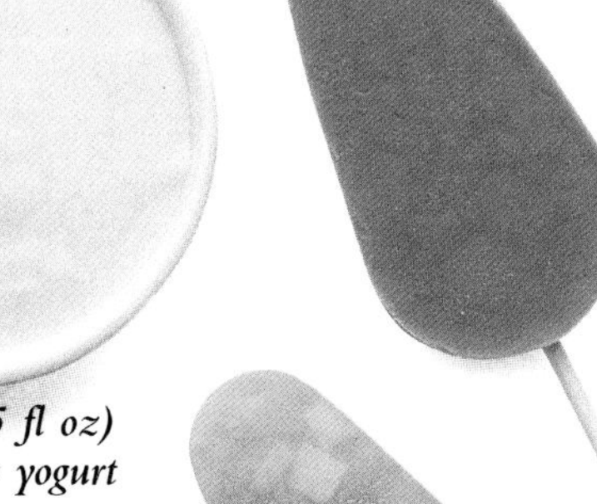

FRUIT LOLLIES

For orange fruit lolly

100 ml (4 fl oz) orange and apricot juice

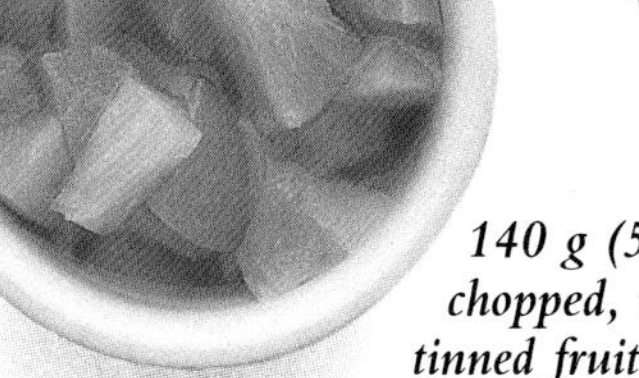

140 g (5 oz) chopped, mixed tinned fruit

COOK'S TOOLS

Ice lolly moulds and sticks
Chopping board • Sharp knife • Spoon
Bowl • Measuring jug

Fruity yogurt lolly

Mix the yogurt and blackcurrant syrup together, then pour the mixture into the lolly moulds and put them in the freezer.

Orange fruit lolly

Drain the fruit and put it in a bowl. Mix in the fruit juice, then pour the mixture into the moulds and put in the freezer.

To remove the lollies from the moulds, hold them upside down under a warm tap for a few seconds and gently ease them out.

POPCORN

Making popcorn is like a magic trick and it tastes good! You can buy popping corn from big supermarkets or health-food shops. Serve it warm with melted butter and add salt or sugar, depending on how you like it.

COOK'S TOOLS

Big saucepan with a lid
Wooden spoon

You will need (for 4 servings)

2 tablespoons vegetable oil

55 g (2 oz) popping corn

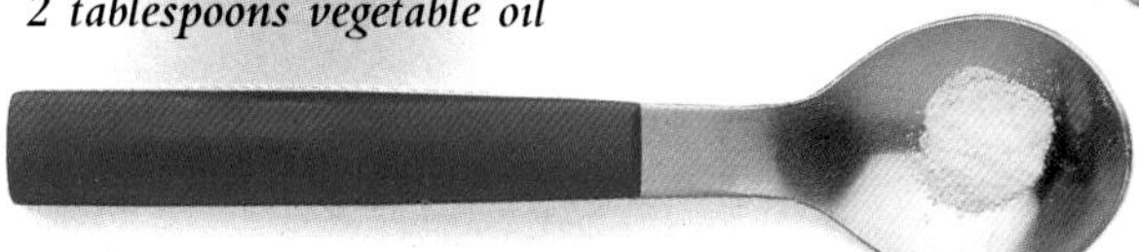

A big pinch of salt

30 g (1 oz) butter

30 g (1 oz) brown sugar (if liked)

POPCORN

Why not use a piping bag as a cone?

What to do

1 Heat the vegetable oil in the saucepan until hot. Then add enough corn to cover the bottom of the pan in a single layer.

2 Cook the corn until it starts to pop, then put the lid on the pan and cook the corn for three minutes, shaking the pan.

3 Take the lid off the pan, add butter and salt or sugar, and stir the popcorn. Then eat it at once.

MILKSHAKES

Here is a recipe for a scrumptious banana milkshake. You can also make it in other flavours – just leave out the banana and use the alternatives shown below to make a raspberry or chocolate shake. There is enough for one large milkshake.

COOK'S TOOLS

Chopping board • Blender
Knife • Spoon

You will need (for 1 large milkshake)

1 tablespoon vanilla ice-cream

1 tablespoon honey

150 ml (1/4 pint) milk

85 g (3 oz) natural yogurt

For banana milkshake

1 banana

For chocolate milkshake

85 g (3 oz) chocolate-flavoured biscuits

For raspberry milkshake

85 g (3 oz) raspberries

What to do

1 Peel and slice the banana. If you are making a chocolate milkshake, break the biscuits up into large pieces.

2 Put all the ingredients for the milkshake into the *blender*, put the lid on and whizz it for about one minute.

3 Take the top off the blender. The milkshake should be evenly mixed and creamy. Put it straight into a tall glass.

Snack in a drink

Serve the milkshakes with straws. If you like, you can decorate the shakes with sliced bananas, grated chocolate, or raspberries.

CHOCOLATE SHAKE

RASPBERRY DREAM

BANANA SHAKE

Eggs and Cheese

Eggs and cheese are key ingredients in cooking. In this part of the book you can learn how to prepare tasty breakfast and tea dishes, such as scrambled eggs, cheese on toast, and savoury tarts. Below is a basic guide to choosing eggs and different sorts of cheese.

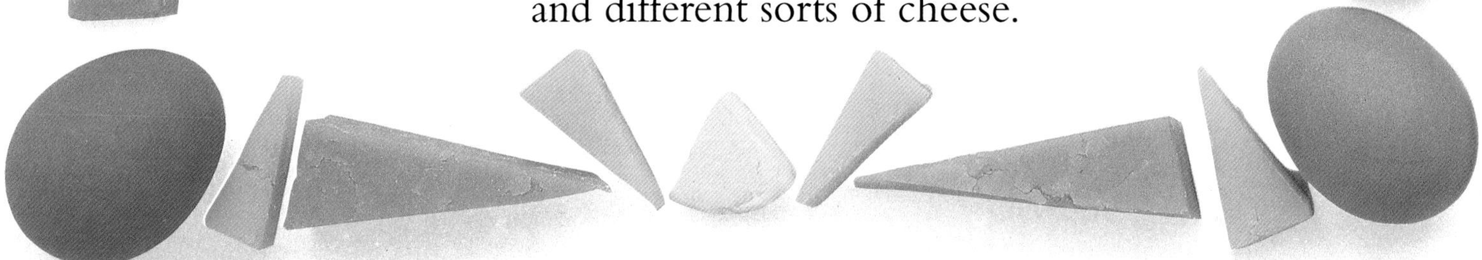

Eggs

The eggs used in recipes in this book are hens' eggs. They are graded by size. We have used Size 2 eggs. Check the date on the box to make sure the eggs are fresh.

Eggs

Cream cheese

Soft cheeses

These range from creamy cheeses like French fromage frais, to semi-soft cheeses, like Greek Feta.

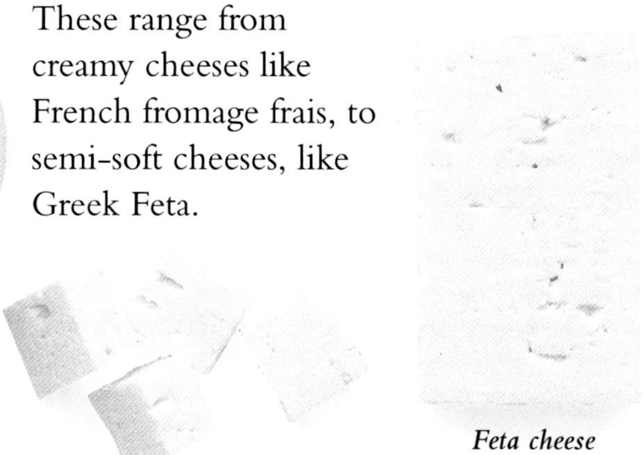

Feta cheese

Fromage frais

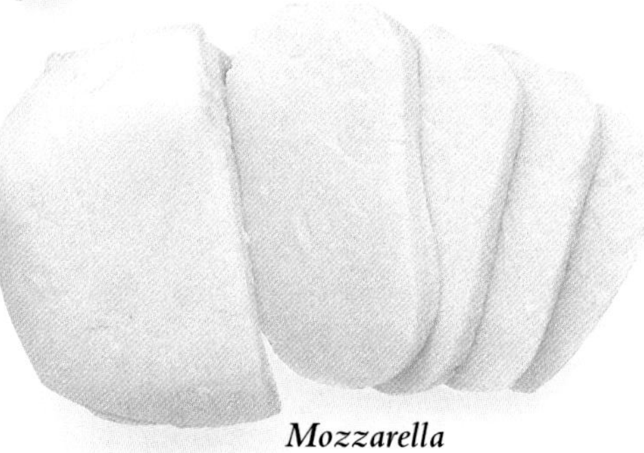

Mozzarella

HARD CHEESES

These cheeses are firm, with a strong flavour and are the ones most often used for flavouring in cooking. They are usually *grated* before being added to other ingredients. When sliced, they are delicious eaten with crusty bread or biscuits.

Parmesan

Grated Parmesan

Cheddar

Red Leicester

Gruyère

Sliced Cheddar

Sliced Red Leicester

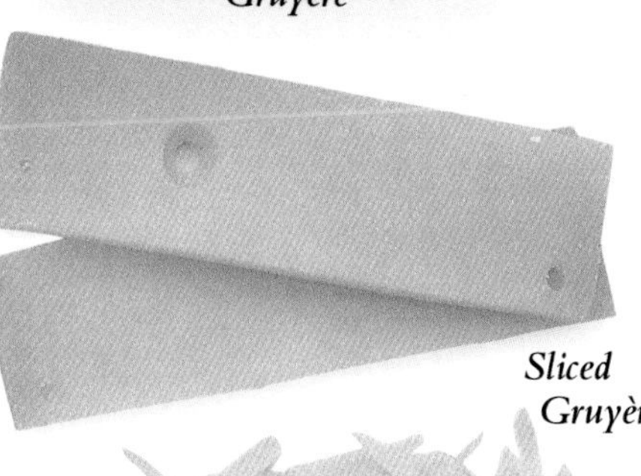

Sliced Gruyère

Grated Cheddar

Grated Red Leicester

Grated Gruyère

SPECIAL CHEESES

Cheeses like this are usually eaten with bread or biscuits. Each of them has a special flavour of its own. Choose two or three contrasting cheeses to serve on a cheeseboard.

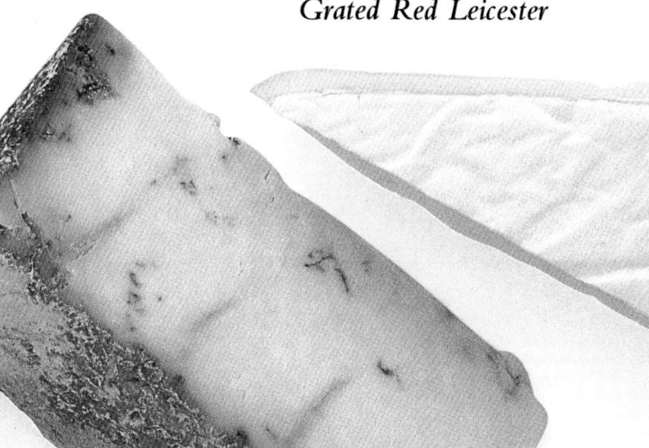

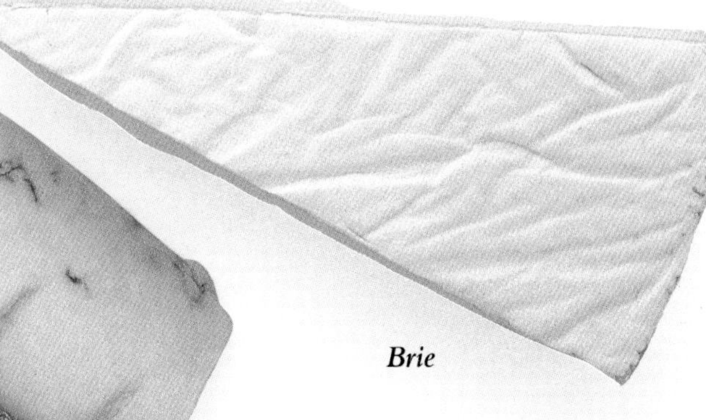

Brie

Crottin (small goat's cheese)

Stilton (blue cheese)

As with all cheeses, buy these cut fresh rather than wrapped in plastic.

SIMPLE EGGS

Boiled eggs are about the easiest thing to cook, and make a delicious breakfast or quick meal. Eat them hot with a little salt and pepper and buttered bread or toast. Hard-boiled eggs are useful for picnics or for adding to salads.

COOK'S TOOLS

Big spoon • Saucepan
Small bowl

You will need (for 3 servings)

BOILED EGGS

What to do

1 Heat some water in a saucepan until it is *simmering*. Then lower the eggs into the water on a big spoon.

2 Boil the eggs for 6 to 7 minutes, then lift them out of the pan. To hard-boil eggs, cook them for 10 to 12 minutes.

3 Put hard-boiled eggs in a bowl of cold water. Tap each one against the bowl to crack its shell, then peel off the shells.

EGGS IN POTS

Baked eggs are easy to make and can be a starter or a quick meal. To vary them, you can tuck some cheese, ham, or cooked vegetables under the eggs as a surprise. It is best to bake eggs in the small, straight-sided dishes called ramekins.

COOK'S TOOLS

Baking tray • Teaspoon
Cheese grater • Ramekins

You will need (for 3 servings)

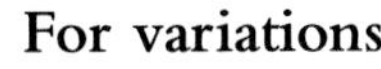

For variations

30 g (1 oz) grated cheese

1 egg per person

3 tablespoons single cream

Pepper

Salt

45 g ($1^{1}/_{2}$ oz) cooked spinach

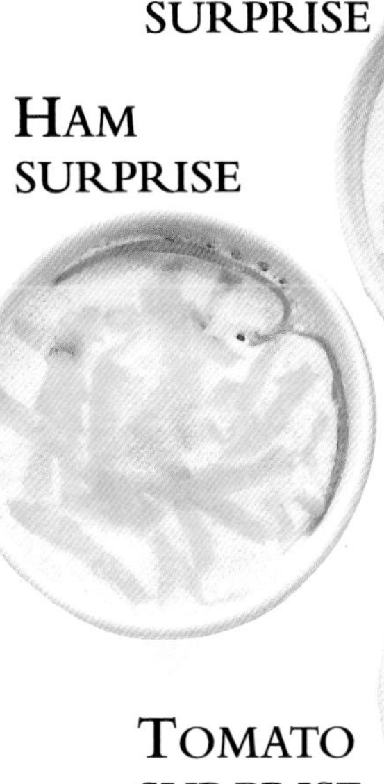

or 30 g (1 oz) tomato sauce

or 1 slice garlic sausage or ham

SPINACH SURPRISE

HAM SURPRISE

TOMATO SURPRISE

What to do

1 Set the oven to 190°C/375°F Gas Mark 5. Butter the ramekins and put in the cooked spinach, tomato sauce, or ham.

2 Add salt and pepper if liked, then break an egg into each ramekin. Spoon the cream on top and add the *grated* cheese.

3 Stand the ramekins on the baking tray and bake them for 15 to 25 minutes, until the whites of the eggs are firm.

SCRAMBLED EGGS

This is one of the simplest, yet most delicious ways of cooking eggs. The secret to making good scrambled eggs is to cook them over a very low heat and to keep stirring them. They should take about five minutes to cook.

COOK'S TOOLS

Chopping board
Bowl • Wooden spoon • Fork
Sharp knife • Saucepan

You will need (for one serving)

For basic scrambled egg

A knob of butter

2 tablespoons milk

2 eggs

A pinch of pepper

A pinch of salt

For ham scramble

55 g (2 oz) cooked, smoked ham

Small sprig of parsley

For Spanish scramble

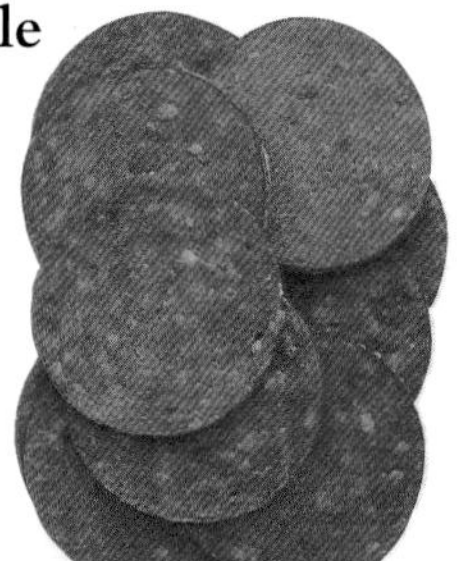

1 tablespoon vegetable oil

30 g (1 oz) sliced peperoni

1/4 red pepper and 1/4 green pepper

Basic scrambled eggs

1 Break the eggs into the bowl. Add the milk, salt, and pepper and *beat* everything together until well mixed.

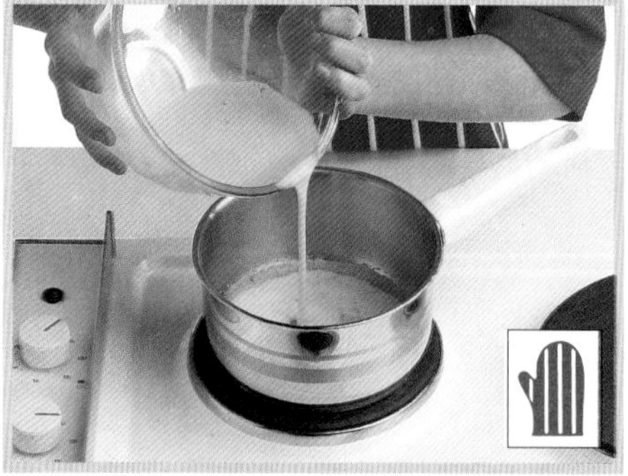

2 Melt the butter in the saucepan over a low heat until foaming. Swirl it round the pan, then pour in the eggs.

3 Cook the eggs over a low heat, stirring them as they begin to thicken. They are ready when creamy and nearly set.

Spanish scramble

1 *Slice* the peppers finely. Then heat the oil in the saucepan and cook the peppers in it for a few minutes.

2 Add the peppers and peperoni to the basic egg mixture. Cook the eggs as before in a saucepan with melted butter.

Ham scramble

Cut the ham into cubes and *chop* the parsley. Add the ham and parsley to the basic egg mixture and cook the eggs as before.

Creamy eggs

Serve the eggs straight away while hot. Garnish them with toast or fried bread cut into shapes with biscuit cutters.

HAM SCRAMBLE

SPANISH SCRAMBLE

Diamond-shaped pieces of toast

Chicken-shaped piece of toast

BASIC SCRAMBLED EGGS

FRENCH TOAST AND CINNAMON TOAST

Here you can find out how to make French toast (sometimes called eggy bread) and cinnamon toast, which is a sweet version of it. Neither is really toast, but fried bread. They make a wonderful teatime treats.

COOK'S TOOLS

Bowl • Frying pan • Biscuit cutter
Fish slice • Fork

You will need

(for 2-3 servings)

One egg for each type of toast

3 slices of bread for each egg

For frying

30 g (1 oz) butter

1 tablespoon vegetable oil

For French toast

Large pinches of salt and pepper

For cinnamon toast

1 teaspoon ground cinnamon

2 tablespoons golden or fine demerara sugar

French toast

1 Break an egg into the bowl. Add the salt and pepper and *beat* the egg with a fork until it is evenly mixed and frothy.

2 Dip each slice of bread into the beaten egg, so that the bread is evenly coated with egg on both sides.

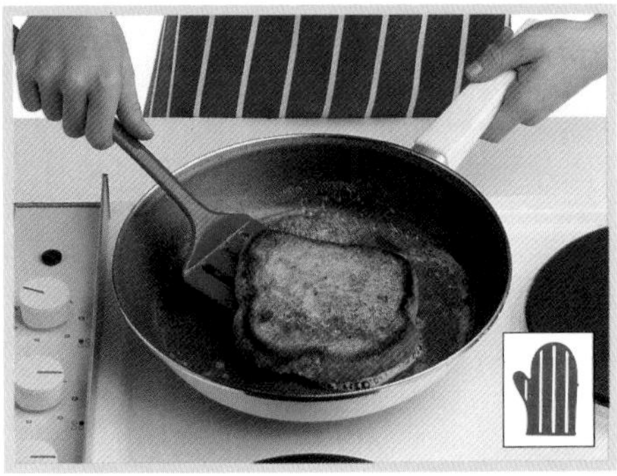

3 Heat the butter and oil in the frying pan. When the pan is hot, fry the bread on both sides until it is golden brown.

Cinnamon toast

1 Cut stars out of the sliced bread with the biscuit cutter. Press the cutter down on the bread, then lift out the stars.

2 Break the egg into the bowl and add the ground cinnamon and half of the sugar. *Beat* the egg with a fork and dip the stars in it.

3 Heat the butter and oil in the frying pan and fry the stars for about 2 to 3 minutes on each side until they are crisp and brown.

FRENCH TOAST

CINNAMON TOAST

Cut the French toast into chunky triangles

Tangy tomato sauce or ketchup to go with the French toast

Sprinkle the remaining sugar onto the cinnamon stars once they have cooled a little

TOASTY TREATS

Grilled cheese on toast is a tasty quick snack or easy meal. Why not have fun and turn it into something special by using different sorts of bread and cheese and by inventing different toppings? Here are some ideas to try.

COOK'S TOOLS

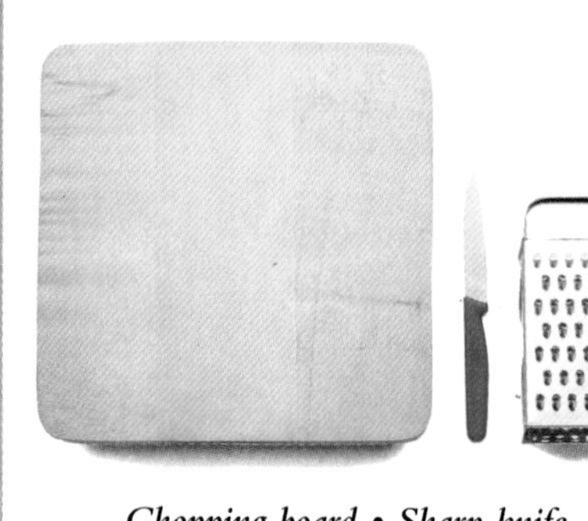

Chopping board • Sharp knife Cheese grater

You will need

(for 1 serving of each toast)

For apple toast

A slice of French bread

15 g (1/2 oz) grated cheese

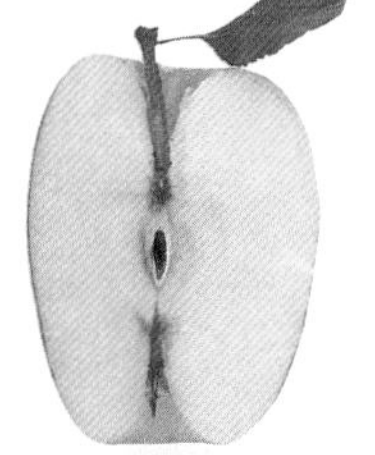

1/4 red apple

A knob of butter

For noughts and crosses

A slice of brown bread

Narrow strips of ham

A slice of cheese

A stoned black olive

Strips of contrasting cheese

For the flower pizza

1/2 teaspoon finely chopped red onion

Half a round roll

30 g (1 oz) grated Mozzarella cheese

2 small tomatoes

2 tiny mushrooms

1 teaspoon grated cheese

What to do

1 Carefully slice the apple, tomatoes, mushrooms, and olive. Cut the ham into small pieces and *grate* the cheese.

2 Follow the pictures on the opposite page to see how to arrange the different ingredients on each piece of bread.

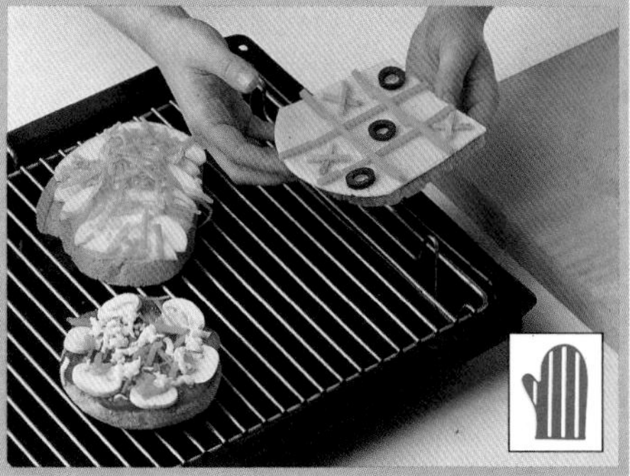

3 Heat the grill until it is hot, then put the pieces of bread on the grill pan and *grill* them until the cheese is bubbling.

Apple toast

1 Toast the French bread lightly, then butter it. Cover it with overlapping slices of apple.

2 Sprinkle a layer of grated cheese over the slices of apple, making sure they are evenly covered.

3 Put the piece of bread under the grill and cook it until the cheese has melted and is bubbling nicely.

Noughts and crosses

1 Turn on the grill and grill the piece of brown bread until it is lightly toasted on one side.

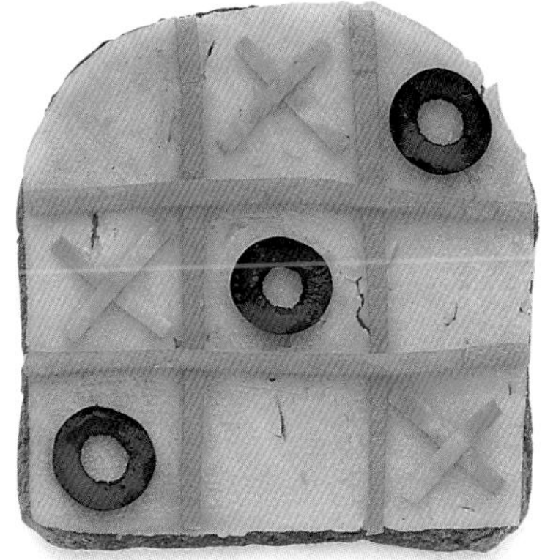

2 Lay a piece of cheese on the untoasted side of the bread. Decorate with the strips of cheese, ham, and slices of olive.

3 Heat the grill and put the toast under it. You will know it is ready when the cheese has melted and is bubbling nicely.

Flower pizza

1 Grate the Mozzarella cheese and lay it on the cut side of the roll. Grill until cheese melts. Arrange sliced tomatoes on top.

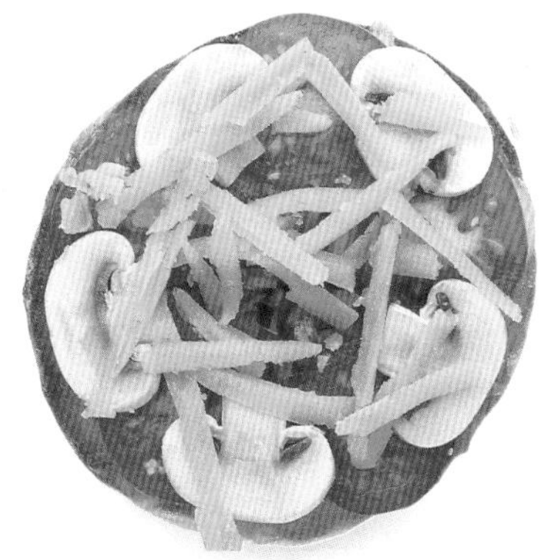

2 Lay sliced mushrooms on the tomatoes and put the chopped onion in the middle of them. Sprinkle with the grated cheese.

3 Put the roll under the heated grill and toast it until the grated cheese has melted and is bubbling.

QUICHES AND TARTS

Making pastry is easy once you know how! Here you can find out how to make a classic Quiche Lorraine or four tiny tarts using the same pastry and basic filling. You will only need half the basic filling for the tiny tarts.

You will need (for 4 servings)

For pastry

115 g (4 oz) plain flour

A pinch of salt

2-3 tablespoons water

30 g (1 oz) butter

30 g (1 oz) lard or white vegetable fat

For basic filling

300 ml ($^1/_2$ pint) cream

2 eggs

Salt and pepper

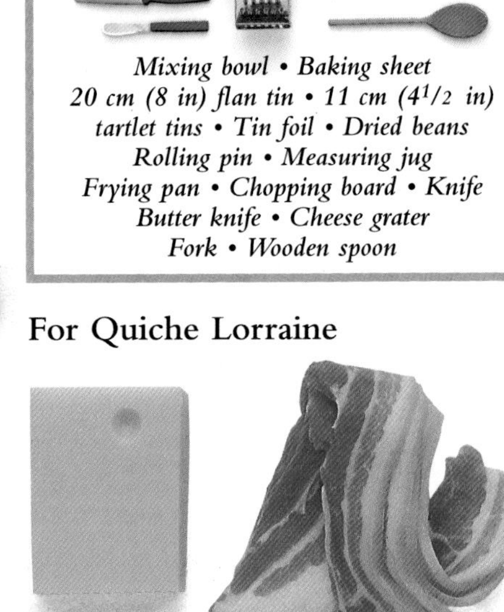

COOK'S TOOLS

Mixing bowl • Baking sheet
20 cm (8 in) flan tin • 11 cm ($4^1/_2$ in) tartlet tins • Tin foil • Dried beans
Rolling pin • Measuring jug
Frying pan • Chopping board • Knife
Butter knife • Cheese grater
Fork • Wooden spoon

For Quiche Lorraine

85 g (3 oz) Gruyère cheese

115 g (4 oz) streaky bacon

What to do

1 Set the oven to 200°C/400°F/Gas Mark 6. Cut up the butter and lard and put them in the bowl with the flour.

2 *Rub* the butter, flour, and lard together with your fingertips until they look like fine breadcrumbs.

3 Mix in the water a little at a time until you have a soft ball of *dough* that leaves the sides of the bowl clean.

For spinach tarts

55 g (2 oz) grated Cheddar cheese

115 g (4 oz) frozen or cooked spinach

4 slices of tomato

2 spring onions

For asparagus tarts

12 cooked, frozen, or canned asparagus tips

55 g (2 oz) grated Gruyère cheese

For tomato and Parmesan tarts

4 tomatoes

55 g (2 oz) grated Parmesan cheese

For courgette and mushroom tarts

7 g (1/4 oz) butter for frying

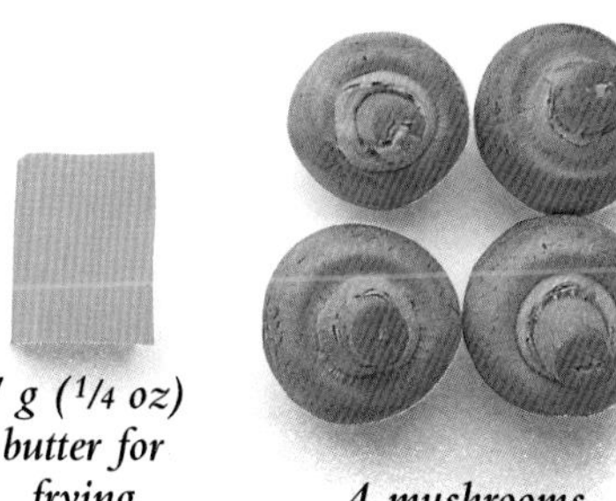

4 mushrooms

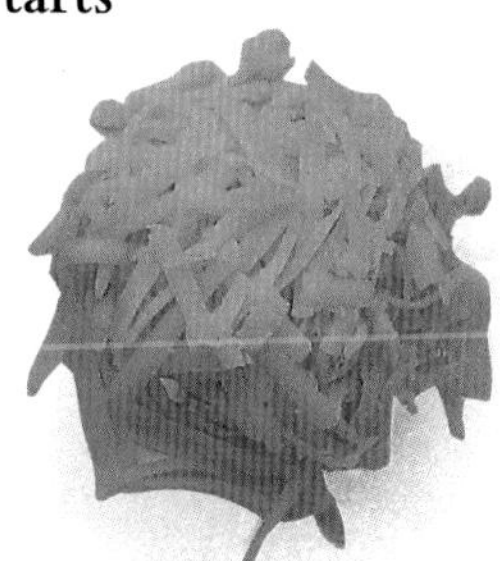

55 g (2 oz) grated Cheddar cheese

1 small courgette

4 Sprinkle flour on the table and on the rolling pin. *Roll* the ball of dough out into a circle until it is quite thin.

5 Check that the pastry is big enough, then lay it in the quiche tin. Press it gently into place and trim the edges.

6 For the tarts, break the dough into four pieces. Roll each piece into a ball, then press it down and roll it out into a circle.

Cooking the pastry

1 Lay each circle of pastry over a tart tin and press it into place. Roll the rolling pin over it to trim the edges of pastry.

2 Line each pastry case with a piece of tin foil and fill it with dried beans. *Bake* the pastry cases for 15 minutes.

3 Then take the pastry cases out of the oven. Let them cool for a minute, then carefully lift out the tin foil and beans.

Filling the quiche

1 Chop the bacon into small cubes and fry it quickly in the frying pan until crisp. Spread the bacon across the pastry.

2 Break the eggs into a jug. Add the cream, salt, and pepper and *beat* them together with a fork. *Grate* the cheese.

3 Pour the egg mixture over the bacon and sprinkle the cheese on top. Bake the quiche for about 25 minutes until firm.

Filling the tarts

1 Slice the mushrooms and tomatoes. Cut the courgettes into short sticks and chop the spring onions finely.

2 Arrange the fillings inside the pastry cases. Mix one egg, 150 ml ($^{1}/_{4}$ pint) cream, salt, and pepper together in a jug.

3 Pour the egg mixture into the tart cases and sprinkle cheese on top. Bake the tarts for about 15 minutes until firm and set.

All in a pastry case

You can eat the quiche and tarts hot or cold. They taste very good served with tiny new potatoes and green salad.

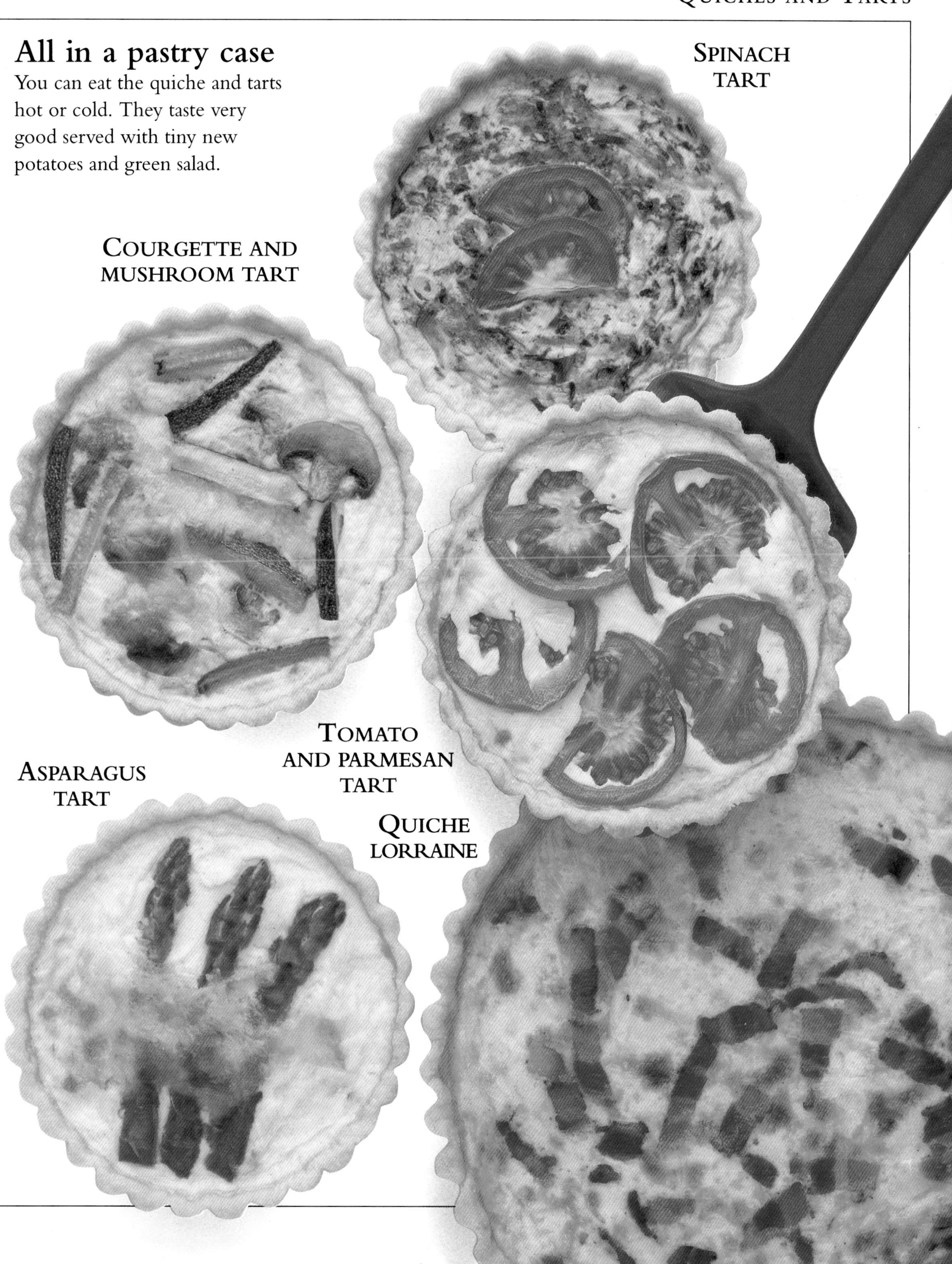

SPINACH TART

COURGETTE AND MUSHROOM TART

TOMATO AND PARMESAN TART

ASPARAGUS TART

QUICHE LORRAINE

PASTA, RICE, AND PIZZA

In this part of the book you can learn how to make some delicious, filling meals all based on pasta, rice, and pizza. There are many different kinds of rice and pasta, and an endless variety of simple, tasty ways to prepare them. Some of the many types available are listed below.

RICE

Long grain rice is used for savoury dishes and short grain rice for risottos and puddings. Wholegrain rice is brown. White rice has had the outer husks of the grain removed. It is less healthy than brown rice but it cooks more quickly.

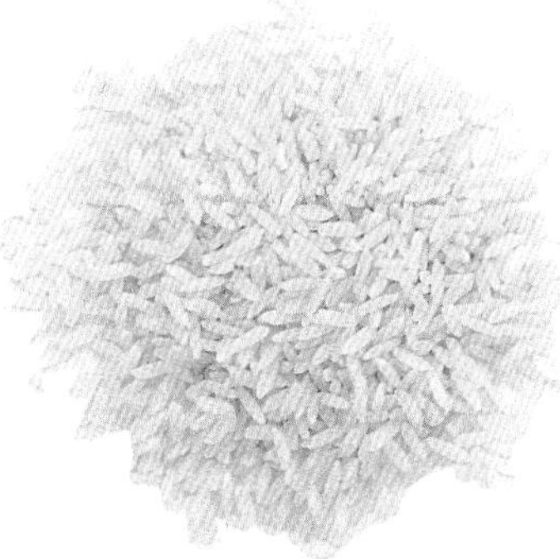

White long grain rice

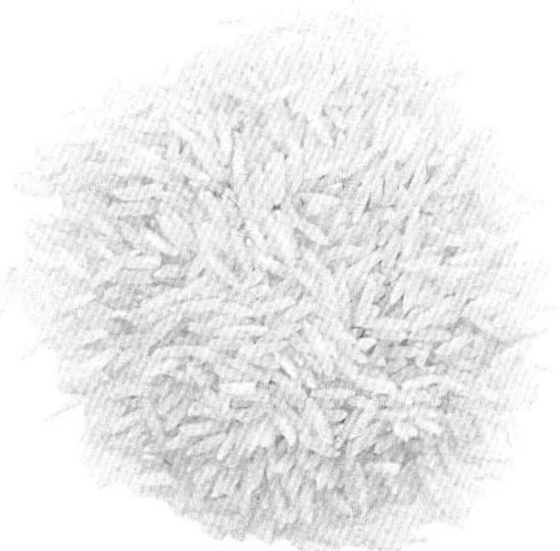

Basmati rice

Pudding rice

Long wholegrain rice

White short grain rice

PASTA

Pasta comes either fresh or dried. Dried pasta takes 10 to 20 minutes to cook and fresh pasta three minutes. Plain pasta made with white flour is yellow. Wholemeal pasta is brown. Green pasta has spinach added to it, red pasta tomato paste, and pink pasta beetroot juice.

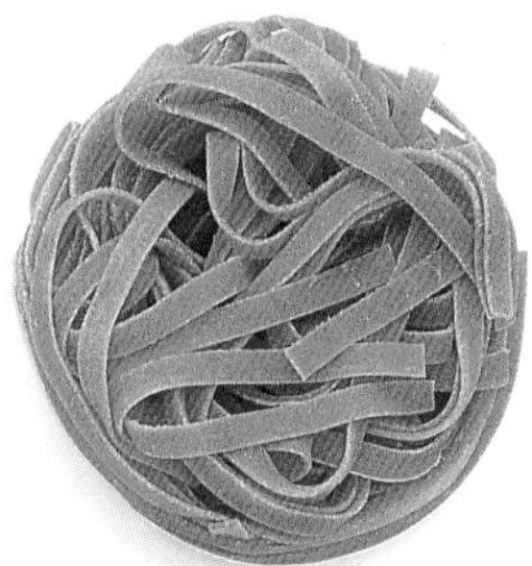

Dried tomato tagliatelle

FLAT PASTA

Pasta also comes in all shapes and sizes, each shape with its own Italian name. Spaghetti and tagliatelle are two types of long, ribbon pasta. Lasagne are wide ribbons of pasta used for baked dishes of layered pasta - called lasagne!

Fresh green tagliatelle

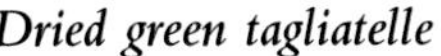

Dried green tagliatelle

Fresh tagliatelle

Green lasagne

Wholemeal spaghetti

Plain spaghetti

Green spaghetti

White lasagne

Wholemeal lasagne

TUBE PASTA

You can buy dried pasta in many different-shaped tubes, ranging from small macaroni to large, ribbed rigatoni or penne. These types of pasta are good served with rich, chunky, meat sauces.

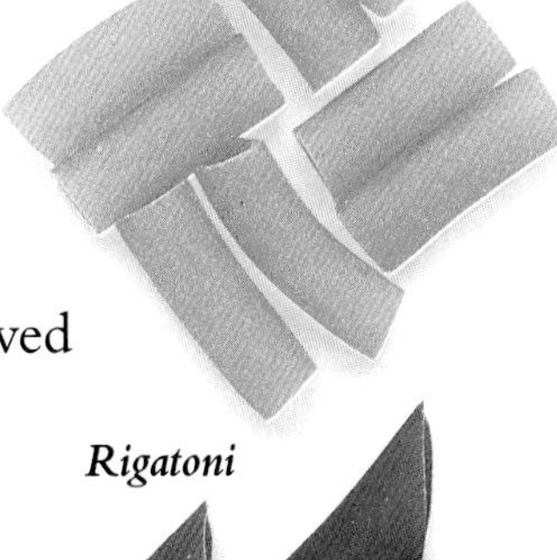

Rigatoni

INTERESTING SHAPES

Pasta bows, shells, and twists fall into this group, along with lots of other unusual shapes. The smaller shapes are sometimes used in soups. The larger ones can be served with any sauce.

Shells (conchiglie)

Macaroni

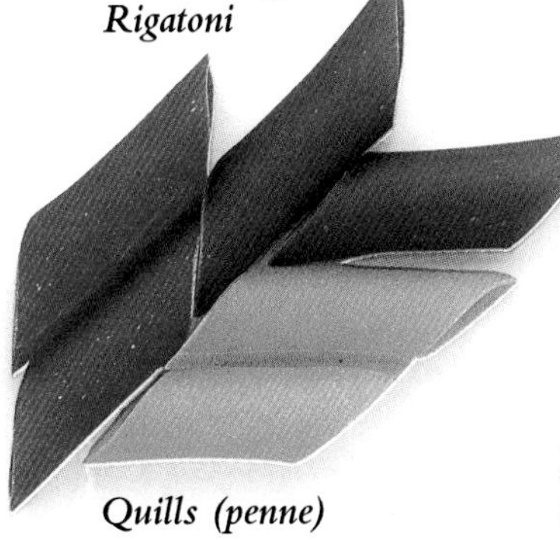

Quills (penne)

Bows (farfalle)

Twists (fusilli)

CREAMY SPAGHETTI

Here you can learn how to cook pasta (spaghetti in this case) and see how to turn it into a delicious quick meal, by adding a few ingredients. This recipe is for a carbonara sauce. Turn the page to find out how to make tomato and Bolognese sauces for pasta.

COOK'S TOOLS

Frying pan • Wooden spoon
Chopping board • Fork
Cheese grater • Large saucepan
Small bowl • Colander

You will need (for 4 servings)

340 g (12 oz) spaghetti or other long pasta

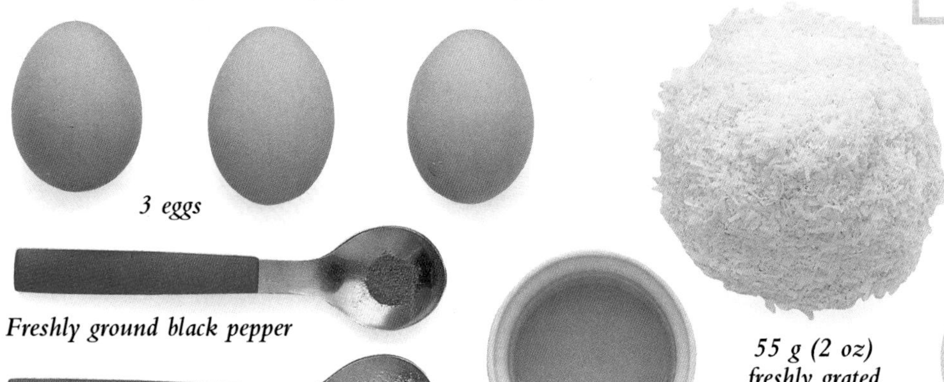

3 eggs

Freshly ground black pepper

A pinch of salt

55 g (2 oz) freshly grated Parmesan cheese

1 1/2 tablespoons vegetable oil

115 g (4 oz) chopped streaky bacon

2 tablespoons double cream

What to do

1 Heat some water in a big saucepan. Add a pinch of salt and a drop of oil to stop the pasta sticking together.

2 When the water boils, gently push the pasta into the water until covered. Long pasta slides down as the ends soften.

3 While the pasta cooks, *beat* the eggs in a bowl. Add the cream, salt, pepper, and half the cheese and beat again.

4 Put the oil in the frying pan. Add the chopped bacon and fry it quickly for a few minutes until it is cooked.

5 Cook the pasta for about 12 to 15 minutes until it is cooked but still firm. Then tip it into a colander and drain it well.

6 Tip the pasta back into the saucepan. Add the egg mixture and bacon. Stir well and cook it for a few more minutes.

Creamy pasta

Put the spaghetti carbonara in a serving dish and sprinkle the rest of the grated Parmesan cheese on top. Then eat it straight away while it is piping hot.

Grated Parmesan cheese

Bacon

PASTA SAUCES

Here are two classic pasta sauces – tomato sauce and Bolognese sauce – which you can make from the same basic recipe. Serve them with 340 g (12 oz) pasta for four people. Make the sauce first and cook the pasta last when you are ready to eat.

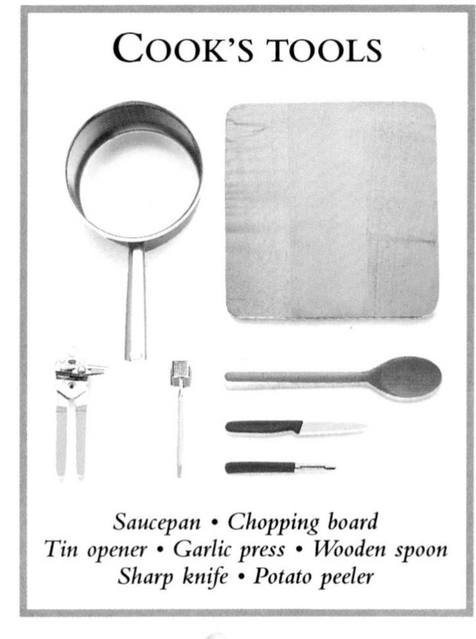

COOK'S TOOLS

Saucepan • Chopping board
Tin opener • Garlic press • Wooden spoon
Sharp knife • Potato peeler

You will need (for 4 servings)

1 stick celery

1 small carrot

1 clove garlic

A 400 g (14 oz) tin of tomatoes

1/2 teaspoon salt

1/2 teaspoon pepper

3 tablespoons tomato purée

2 tablespoons olive oil

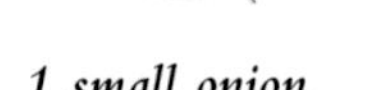

1 small onion

For tomato sauce

150 ml (1/4 pint) water

For Bolognese sauce

3 rashers streaky bacon

340 g (12 oz) minced beef

Tomato sauce

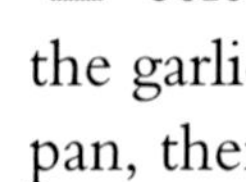

1 *Chop* the onion, carrot, and celery finely. Peel and *crush* the garlic. Heat the oil in the pan, then add the vegetables.

2 Cook the vegetables gently for about 5 minutes, until soft. Add the tomatoes, tomato purée, and water and stir.

3 Let the sauce *simmer* for about 45 minutes, stirring it from time to time. Taste it, and add salt and pepper if needed.

Bolognese sauce

1 Chop the vegetables and bacon. Heat the oil in the pan and cook the vegetables for about 5 minutes.

2 Add the minced meat and chopped bacon. Cook until the meat has browned, stirring all the time.

3 Stir in the tinned tomatoes and tomato purée. Heat the sauce up, then let it simmer gently for 45 minutes.

Saucy meals

Different sauces suit different types of pasta. Bolognese sauce goes best with long pasta like spaghetti or tagliatelle. Delicately flavoured tomato sauce, however, is best with small, chunky pasta. Sprinkle with Parmesan cheese for extra flavour.

PASTA WITH BOLOGNESE SAUCE

Sprinkle with Parmesan cheese

PASTA WITH TOMATO SAUCE

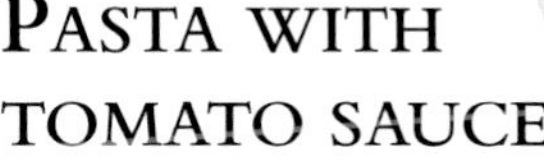

This squiggly pasta is known as orrecchiette which means "little ears" in Italian.

VEGETABLES AND RICE

Learn the basic method for cooking rice and see how to use it as the base for a wonderful meal. Prepare the vegetables while the rice is cooking, then keep the rice warm while you quickly fry the vegetables over a high heat – it's delicious!

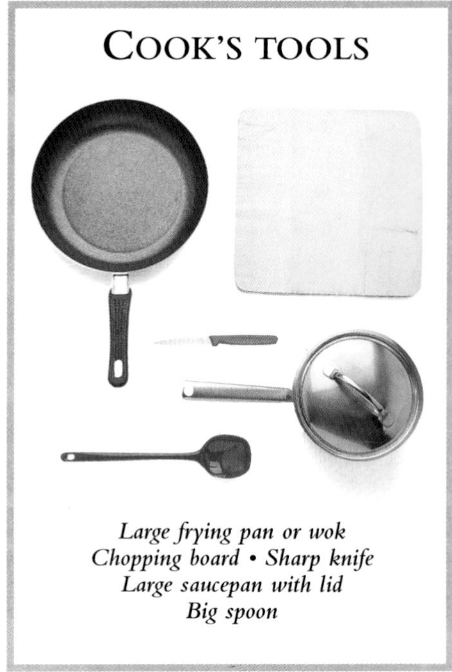

COOK'S TOOLS

Large frying pan or wok
Chopping board • Sharp knife
Large saucepan with lid
Big spoon

You will need

(for 4 servings)

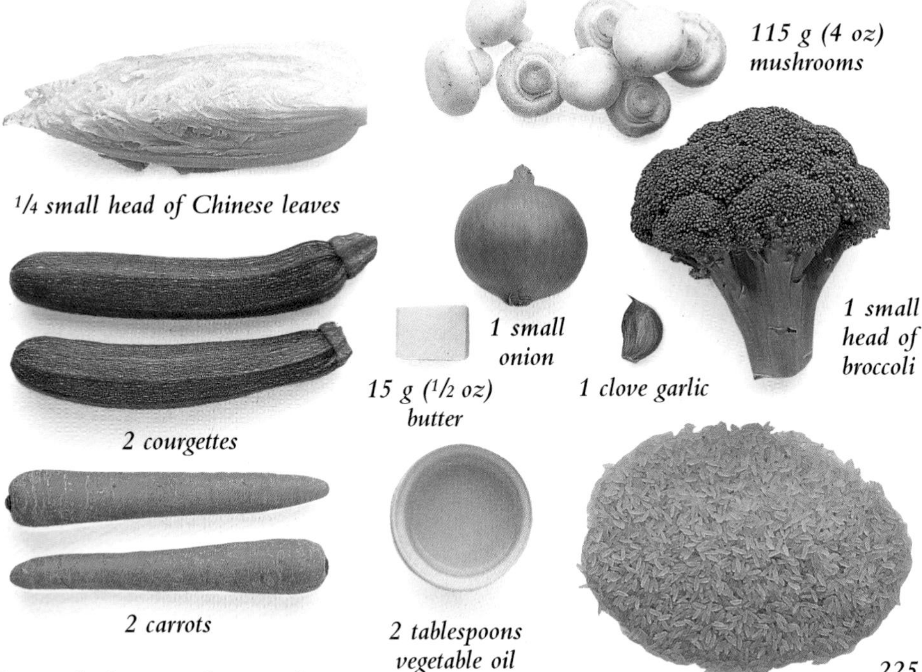

1/4 small head of Chinese leaves
115 g (4 oz) mushrooms
2 courgettes
1 small onion
15 g (1/2 oz) butter
1 clove garlic
1 small head of broccoli
2 carrots
2 tablespoons vegetable oil
225 g (8 oz) long grain rice

1-2 tablespoons soy sauce
450 ml (3/4 pint) water
1 teaspoon salt

Cooking the rice

1 Melt the butter in a big saucepan over a low heat. Add the rice, stir well, and cook for a few minutes until it is transparent.

2 Add the water and salt and put a lid on the pan. Let the rice cook gently for about 15 minutes without stirring it.

3 The rice is cooked when it is tender and has absorbed all the water. Bite a few grains to check whether it is done.

Preparing the vegetables

4 Cut the courgettes and carrots into sticks. *Slice* the onion, mushrooms, and Chinese leaves, and cut up the broccoli.

5 Heat the oil in the frying pan. Add the onion, crushed garlic, carrots, and broccoli, and stir over a high heat for 5 minutes or so.

6 Add the other vegetables and stir them over a high heat until just tender. Pour the soy sauce into the pan and stir well.

Vegetables on a bed of rice

Turn the rice out on to a serving dish. Spread it out, then arrange the stir-fried vegetables on top and serve the meal at once while hot.

CHINESE FRIED RICE

This wonderful fried rice is a meal on its own and only takes about ten minutes to cook, once everything is prepared. You can vary the recipe by adding other things you like - diced, cooked chicken perhaps, or sliced mushrooms.

COOK'S TOOLS

Large frying pan or Chinese wok
Chopping board • Big spoon • Fork
Sharp knife • Garlic press
Colander • Small bowl
Large saucepan with lid

You will need (to serve 4)

For boiling the rice

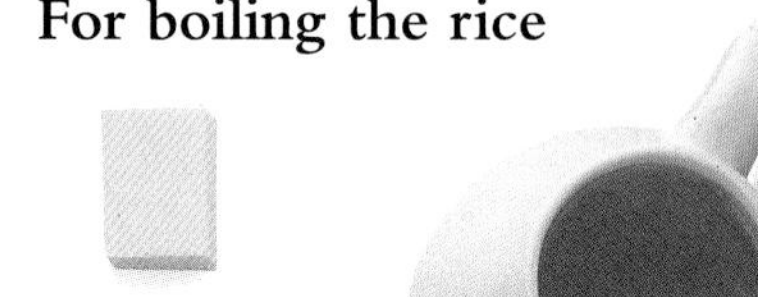

15 g (1/2 oz) butter

450 ml (3/4 pint) water

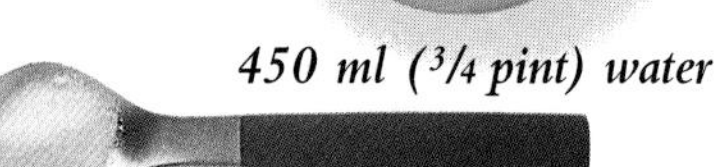

1 teaspoon salt

225 g (8 oz) long grain rice

The remaining ingredients

2 eggs

115 g (4 oz) peas

1/2 teaspoon salt

A small cube of root ginger

1 clove garlic

1/2 small head chinese leaves

225 g (8 oz) prawns

150 ml (1/4 pint) chicken stock

1 tablespoon soy sauce

1 small onion

1 tablespoon vegetable o

What to do

1 Cook the rice as shown on page 46. Cook the peas in boiling, slightly salted water for 5 minutes, then drain them.

2 *Peel* the ginger and chop it finely. Peel and *crush* the garlic. *Slice* the onion and the Chinese leaves.

3 Heat the oil in a large frying pan and *fry* the onion, garlic, and ginger in it gently, stirring constantly for about 5 minutes.

4 Add the sliced Chinese leaves to the frying pan. Cook them over a high heat for about a minute, stirring all the time.

5 Add the rice, stock, and soy sauce, then the prawns and peas. Stir everything together and cook it for a few minutes.

6 *Beat* the eggs. Make a hollow in the rice, pour in the eggs and cook them for a few minutes, then stir them into the rice.

A taste of the East

As this is a meal full of interesting flavours, why not take the oriental theme a bit further. You could serve the rice in bowls and maybe even try using chopsticks!

Prawns

Peas

Sliced Chinese leaves

PIZZA FEAST

You can make scrumptious pizzas using this quick recipe. There are three different toppings to try, or you can experiment with ideas of your own. The quantities given will make four mini-pizzas or one big one.

COOK'S TOOLS

Baking sheet • Mixing bowl
Frying pan • Rolling pin
Chopping board • Sharp knife
Cheese grater • Wooden spoon

You will need
(for 4 servings)

225 g (8 oz) self-raising flour

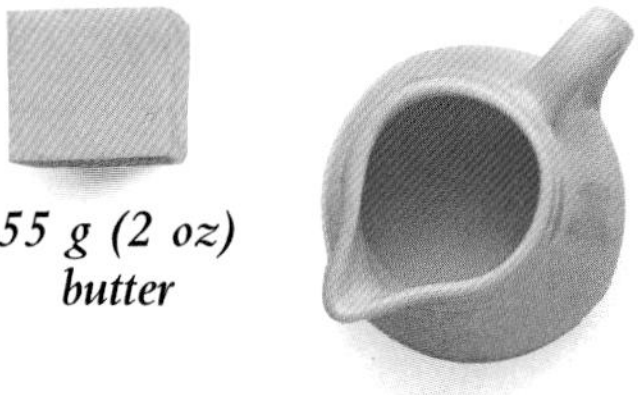

55 g (2 oz) butter

7-8 tablespoons milk

1/2 teaspoon of salt

For the tomato sauce

1 small tin tomatoes

Salt and pepper

1 teaspoon sugar

1 dessertspoon tomato purée

A pinch of oregano or mixed herbs

For the toppings

Stoned black olives

Capers

Grated Cheddar cheese

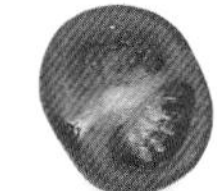

Half a tomato

Sliced courgettes

Sliced mushrooms

Sliced spicy sausage

Sliced peperoni

Finely sliced onions

Chopped ham

Grated Mozzarella cheese

Tinned tuna fish

Tomato sauce

Cook all the ingredients for the tomato sauce together in the frying pan for about 10 minutes to thicken them.

Making the pizza

1 Set the oven to 220°C/ 425°F/Gas Mark 7. *Rub* the flour, salt, and butter together in a mixing bowl.

2 When the mixture looks like breadcrumbs, add the milk and stir everything together into a smooth ball of *dough*.

3 Cut the dough in four and roll each piece into a ball. *Roll* these out into circles about 13 cm (5 in) across.

4 Lay the circles of dough on the greased baking sheet. Spread tomato sauce over them to just within the edges.

5 Add toppings to the pizzas, then *bake* them in the oven for 15 to 20 minutes until the bases are golden brown.

All on a pizza

Choose two or three things that taste good together for the top of each pizza and arrange them as attractively as you can.

TUNA PIZZA

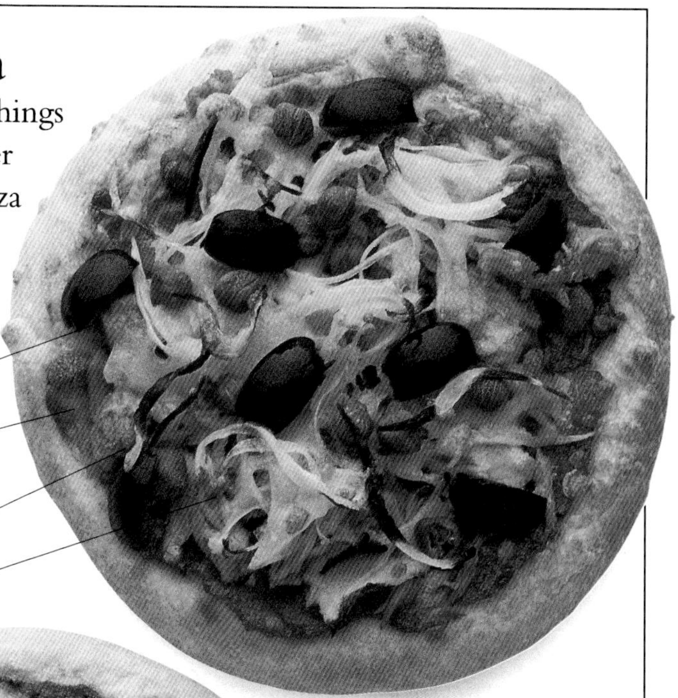

Black olive

Caper

Tinned tuna fish

Sliced onion

SPICY SAUSAGE PIZZA

Chopped ham

Grated Mozzarella cheese

Sliced spicy sausage

Sliced peperoni

COURGETTE PIZZA

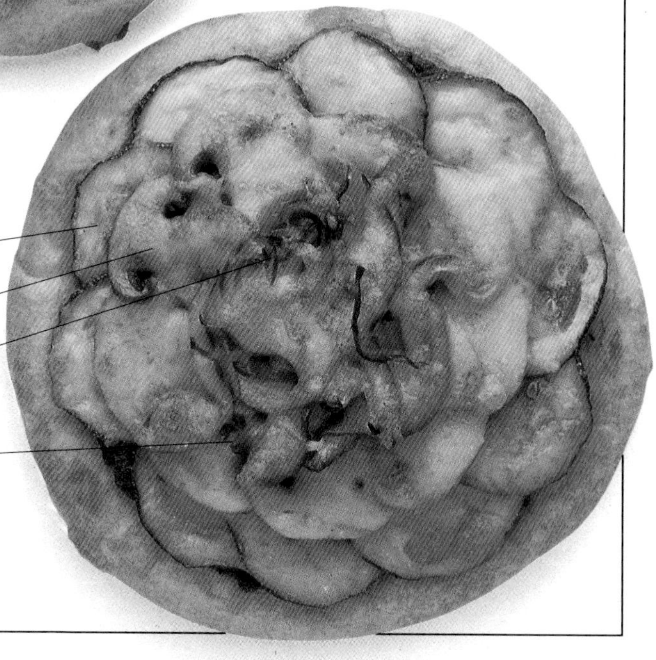

Sliced courgette

Sliced mushroom

Grated cheese

Sliced onion

VEGETABLES

In this part of the book you will find out how to bring out the best in vegetables by cooking them properly. There are many kinds of vegetables available to choose from. You can learn how to create colourful salads and turn the humble potato into a feast fit for a king. Below is a beginner's guide to which vegetables and herbs are which.

HERBS

Adding fresh herbs to salads and cooked vegetables adds extra flavour to them. The herbs shown here are the most useful ones to start with.

Thyme

Bay leaves

Mint

Flat parsley

Chives

Curly parsley

SALAD LEAVES

You can make green salads more interesting by trying out different salad leaves. Use your favourite lettuce as a base and add any of the leaves below.

Rocket

Cos lettuce

Lollo rosso

Frisée (curly endive)

Lamb's lettuce

VEGETABLES

Here are the vegetables used in this book. Buy vegetables when they are in season. Fresh vegetables should be firm and have a good colour.

BEANS

You can make wonderful vegetable stews and salads with beans. Try using tinned beans to start with, as dried beans need to be soaked and take a long time to cook.

Red kidney beans

Haricot beans

Borlotti beans

Avocado

Celery

Chinese leaves

Broccoli

Fresh peas

White onion

Brown onion

Red onion

Garlic

Courgette

Small cucumber

Carrots

Plum tomato

Cherry tomato

Medium tomato

Beefsteak tomato

Red pepper

Orange pepper

Green pepper

Maincrop potato

New potatoes

COOKING VEGETABLES

The key to cooking vegetables is not to overcook them. They should be tender but still be firm when you bite them. Here is a guide to how to prepare and cook some favourite vegetables. To test when they are cooked, push the point of a knife into one of them.

Carrots

Peel big carrots and scrub new ones. Trim the ends off, then slice or cut them into small sticks. Cook them in boiling, salted water for 8 to 10 minutes, then drain and *season* them.

Peas

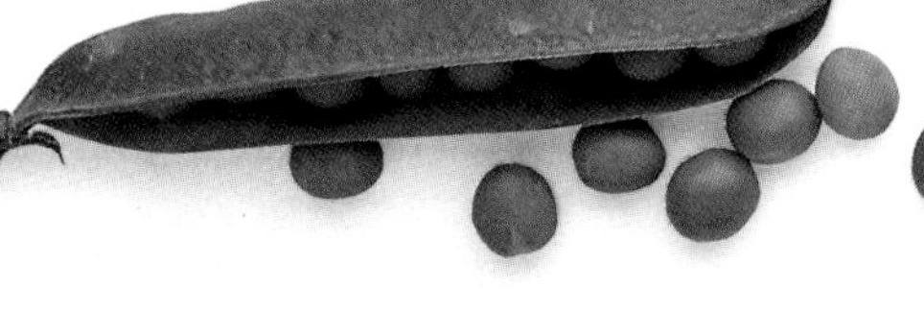

Take the fresh peas out of their pods and cook them in a little boiling, salted water for 5 to 10 minutes. Drain them and add salt, pepper, and a little butter. Frozen peas should be brought to the boil then *simmered* for 3 to 4 minutes.

Cauliflower

Cut the leaves off the cauliflower, cut out the core and cut it into florets. Cook it in boiling, salted water for 5 to 6 minutes until just tender, then drain it and season well.

Broccoli

Cut the thick stem off the broccoli and cut it into small, even-sized florets. Cook it in the same way as cauliflower, stem-side down in the water, or steam it until tender.

Preparing vegetables

1 Wash vegetables in cold water, but do not let them soak. If they are muddy, scrub them with a small brush.

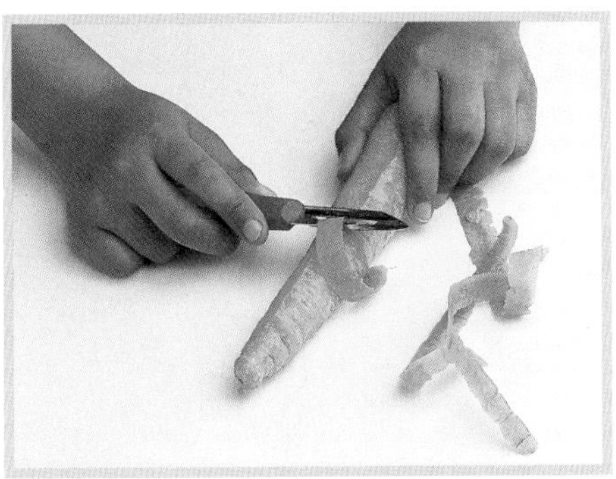

2 New, small vegetables only need to be washed, but it is best to peel larger vegetables which have tougher skins.

3 Slice the ends off the vegetables, cut away any tough stalks, or pick off any damaged leaves. Slice them if they are big.

Mushrooms

Wipe mushrooms clean. Trim the stalks level with the caps and slice the mushrooms vertically. Gently sauté the mushrooms in butter for a few minutes, stirring all the time, until they are tender.

Potatoes

Scrub new potatoes. Peel big potatoes and cut out any eyes (or scrub them, then peel them when cooked). Cook them in boiling, salted water for 12 to 18 minutes until tender.

Green beans

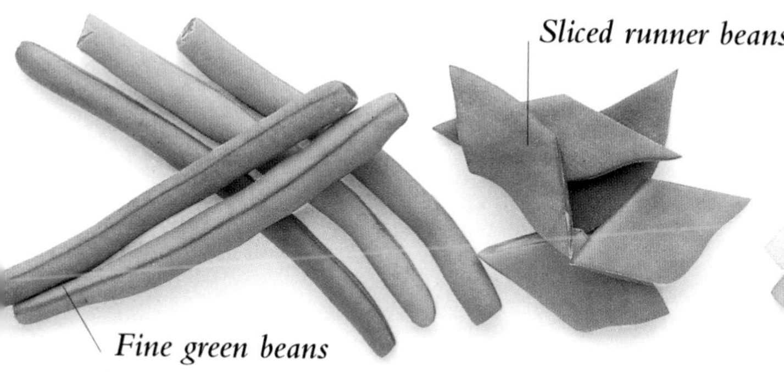

Slice the ends off fine green beans with a pair of scissors. Slice the ends off runner beans, strip away the stringy edge and slice them. Boil or steam both sorts of beans for about 5 minutes, until tender.

Courgettes

Wipe courgettes clean, then cut them into thin rounds or slice them into small sticks. Sauté them gently in a mixture of butter and oil for 5 to 6 minutes until the edges are crisp and brown.

Cooking vegetables

Bring some salted water to the boil in a saucepan. Add the prepared vegetables and *simmer* them gently until tender.

Steaming vegetables

Cook the vegetables in a steamer over a little boiling water. Keep a lid on the pan until the vegetables are done.

Sautéing vegetables

Heat a knob of butter and a little oil in a frying pan and fry the vegetables gently until cooked, stirring them often.

SALAD TIME

Salads can be a light accompaniment to a main course or a meal in themselves. Here you can find out how to make a leafy green side salad and dressing and a main course Greek salad, using the same salad dressing.

COOK'S TOOLS

Salad servers • Chopping board
Sharp knife • Screwtop jar • Salad bowl

You will need (for 4 servings)

For the green salad

For the Greek salad

Parsley

Chives

225 g (8 oz) mixed green salad leaves

1 cos lettuce

1 red onion

1 small cucumber

8 stoned black olives

225 g (8 oz) Feta cheese or other sharp, crumbly cheese

4 big tomatoes

For the dressing

Salt

Pepper

1 teaspoon prepared Dijon-style mustard

1 teaspoon dried mint (for the Greek salad)

3 tablespoons olive oil

1 tablespoon wine vinegar or lemon juice

Green salad

1 Wash and dry the salad leaves, then tear them into a salad bowl. *Chop* the herbs and add them to the leaves.

2 Put all the ingredients for the dressing into the jar. Screw on the lid and shake it until everything is mixed together.

3 When you are ready to eat, pour the dressing on to the salad and mix it until the leaves are coated in dressing.

Greek salad

1 *Shred* the lettuce and put in a salad bowl. Peel and slice the onion. Cut the tomatoes into wedges.

2 *Dice* the cucumber. Cut the cheese into cubes. Put the tomatoes, cheese, cucumber, onions, and olives in the bowl.

3 Make a dressing as for the green salad and add the dried mint. Pour it on the salad and mix everything together well.

Juicy salads

Serve the green salad with grilled meat and fish or after a dish of pasta. The Greek salad makes a wonderful summer meal on its own, served with chunks of crisp bread.

GREEK SALAD

You can use Feta cheese or any crumbly cheese with a good flavour

Olive

Try using different salad leaves, such as frisée, rocket, or lamb's lettuce

GREEN SALAD

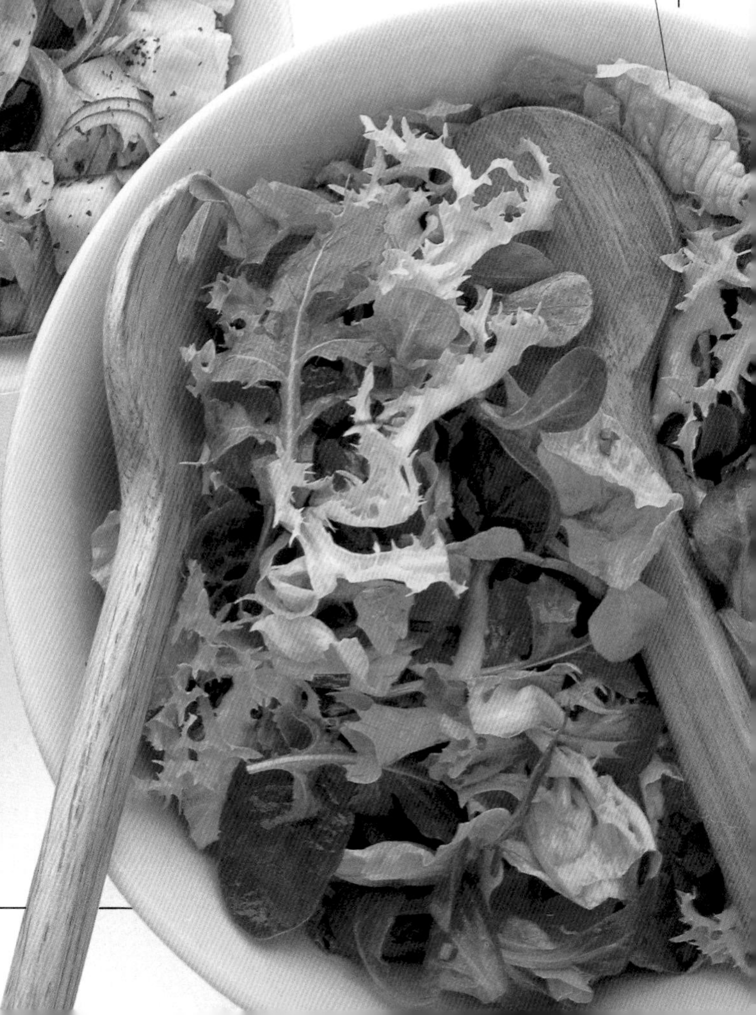

JACKET POTATOES

Stuffed, baked jacket potatoes are one of the easiest things to prepare and make a meal in themselves. Here are four different fillings to try. The ingredients shown are enough to fill one potato, so increase them as needed or invent fillings of your own.

COOK'S TOOLS

Baking sheet • Chopping board
Cheese grater • Spoon
Fork • Sharp knife • Bowl
4 squares of aluminium foil

You will need

(for 4 servings)

4 large potatoes (one per person)

Salt and pepper

Prawn filling

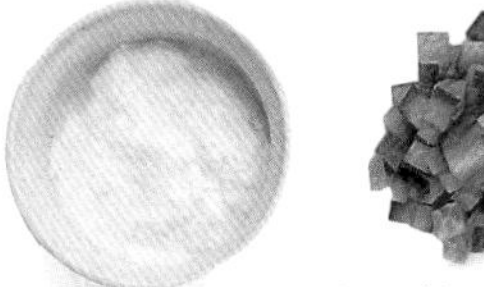

1 tablespoon yogurt

30 g (1 oz) chopped cucumber

30 g (1 oz) prawns

Cheese filling

30 g (1 oz) grated carrot

Half a slice of pineapple

30 g (1 oz) grated cheese

Tuna filling

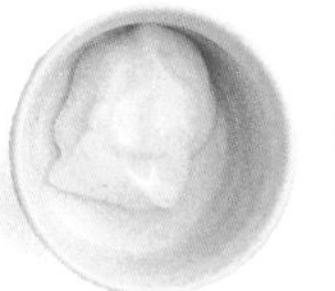

1 tablespoon mayonnaise

30 g (1 oz) cooked sweetcorn

45 g ($1^1/_2$ oz) tinned tuna fish

1 tablespoon chopped spring onion

Ham filling

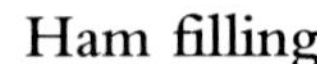

1 slice of chopped ham

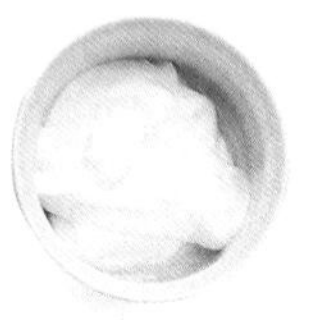

1 tablespoon sour cream

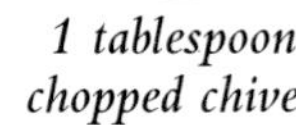

1 tablespoon chopped chives

What to do

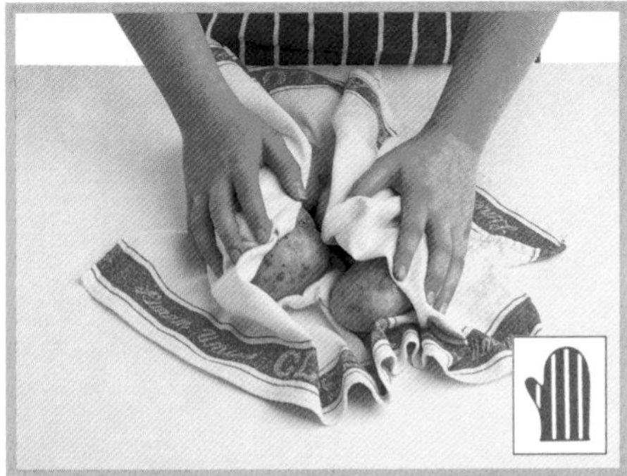

1 Set the oven to 200°C/ 400°F/Gas Mark 6. Scrub the potatoes under a running tap and dry them with a tea towel.

2 Prick the potatoes all over with a fork, then wrap them in foil, put them on a baking sheet, and put them in the oven.

3 The potatoes take 1 to $1^1/_2$ hours to cook. When they are nearly ready, chop and grate the ingredients for the fillings.

4 Then put the ingredients for each filling in a bowl and mix them together. Taste it and add salt and pepper if needed.

5 After an hour, take the potatoes out of the oven. Unwrap one and push a knife into it. If it is soft, it is done.

6 Unwrap the potatoes and make cross-shaped cuts in each of them. Spoon the filling into the cuts in the potatoes.

A meal in a potato

Eat the potatoes straight away while hot. They make a filling meal on their own, or you could serve them with green salad.

HAMMY POTATO

Ham

Chives

CHEESY POTATO

Cheese

Carrot

POTATO WITH PRAWNS

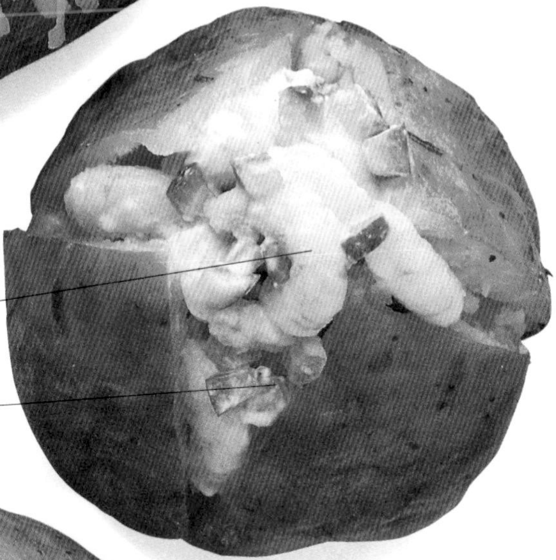

Prawn

Cucumber

TUNA POTATO

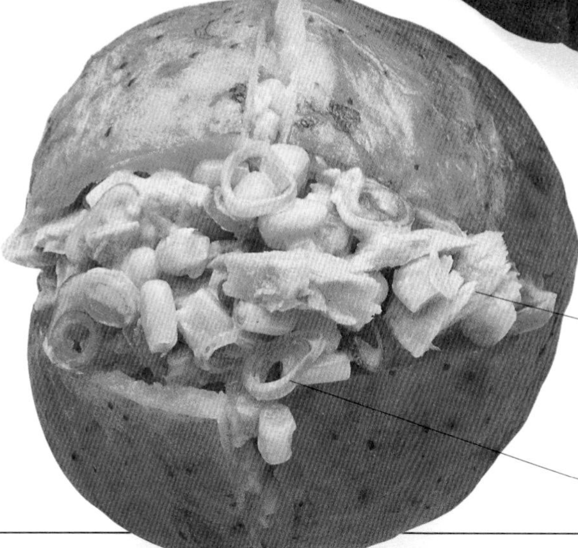

Tuna

Chopped spring onion

CHEESE AND POTATO BAKE

This delicious recipe is useful for a main lunch or supper dish. Or you can leave out the cheese and use it as a vegetable dish to serve with roast meat or ham. It takes one-and-a-half hours to cook, so allow plenty of time.

COOK'S TOOLS

Shallow baking dish • Bowl
Chopping board • Wooden spoon
Fork • Sharp knife • Potato peeler
Cheese grater • Measuring jug
Saucepan

You will need (for 4 servings)

115 g (4 oz) grated Gruyère or strong Cheddar cheese

1 egg

Salt

Freshly ground black pepper

30 g (1 oz) butter

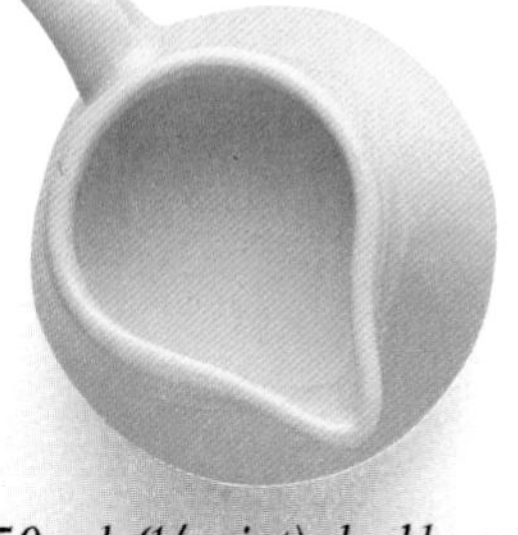

150 ml (1/4 pint) double cream

675 g (1½ lb) medium to large potatoes

1 large onion

What to do

1 Set the oven to 180°C/350°F/Gas Mark 4. Peel the potatoes and slice them finely. Put them in a bowl of water.

2 *Slice* the onion finely. Melt the butter in the saucepan over a low heat and cook the onion until slightly soft.

3 *Grate* the cheese. Butter the baking dish and spread a layer of sliced potatoes on the bottom. Spoon some onions on top.

4 Add salt and pepper, then sprinkle with cheese. Carry on layering potatoes, onions, and cheese, finishing with potatoes.

5 *Beat* the egg into the cream with a fork. Pour it over the potatoes and sprinkle the rest of the cheese on top.

6 *Bake* the potatoes for about 1½ hours. Test them with a knife to check that they are cooked all the way through.

Gold and bubbling

This delicious bake is a good thing to make for vegetarian friends. Decorate it with a sprig of parsley. You could serve it with a green vegetable or follow it with salad.

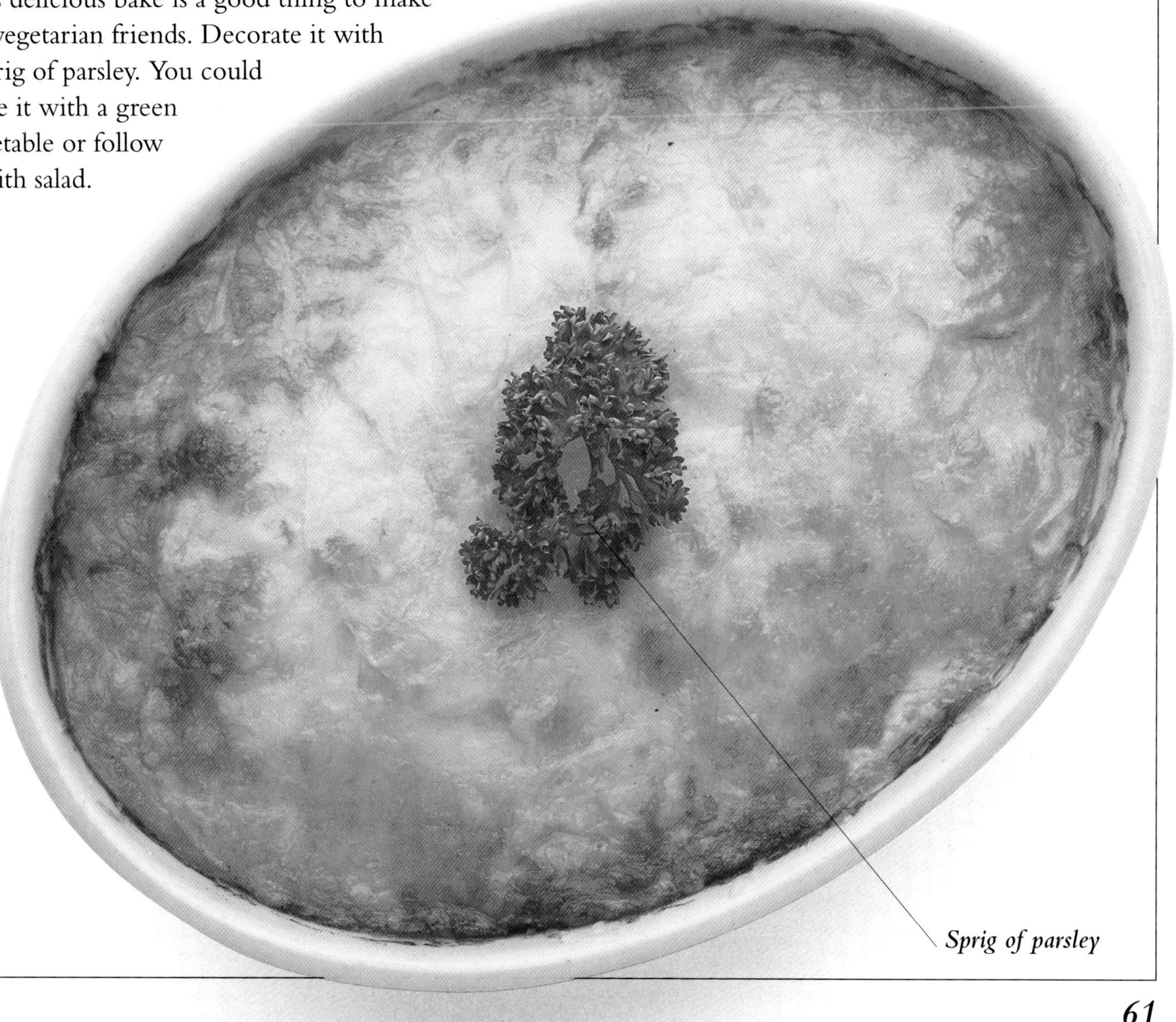

Sprig of parsley

COWBOY BEAN BAKE

Here is a delicious quick version of American baked beans. It's made with tinned beans, but you could cook your own instead if you prefer. You can adapt it for vegetarians by leaving out the bacon and sausages. It is a complete meal in itself.

COOK'S TOOLS

Big saucepan • Chopping board
Tin opener • Sharp knife
Wooden spoon • Colander

You will need (for 4 servings)

1 large onion

400 g (14 oz) tin chopped tomatoes

2 tablespoons oil

225 g (8 oz) spicy sausages (or your favourite sausages)

225 g (8 oz) streaky, smoked bacon

450 g (1 lb) tinned or pre-cooked beans (haricot beans, borlotti, or red kidney beans)

1 tablespoon dark brown sugar

1 teaspoon ready-prepared mustard

A pinch of salt and pepper

What to do

1 Peel the onion and slice it finely. Cut the bacon into small cubes. Cut the sausages into chunky slices.

2 Tip the beans into the colander and drain them well. If they had salt and sugar added to them in the tin give them a rinse.

3 Heat the oil in the saucepan. Cook the onions, bacon, and sausages together until the onions are golden and soft.

4 Add the chopped tomatoes, brown sugar, and mustard and stir. Heat the sauce until it is beginning to bubble.

5 Turn the heat down and let the sauce *simmer* for about half an hour. Stir it now and then to make sure nothing is sticking.

6 Add the drained beans to the sauce and give everything a good stir. Cook for a few more minutes until the beans are hot.

Bean feast

Serve the bean bake with chunks of bread to help mop up any leftover sauce.

Red kidney bean

Haricot bean

Onion

Bacon

Spicy sausage

Borlotti beans

MEAT AND FISH

Meat and fish are the main ingredients in this part of the book. You can learn how to make all sorts of impressive main courses, from grilled kebabs to a rich beef casserole. You must always make sure the meat or fish is fresh. Here is a simple guide to the meat and fish used and the spices which appear throughout the book.

SPICES

Spices are used to add flavour to food. You can buy them ready-ground, or grind your own in a coffee grinder.

Fresh root ginger

Cinnamon sticks

Cayenne *Cloves* *Ground ginger*

Turmeric *Black pepper* *Ground cinnamon*

Sea salt *Curry powder* *Mixed spice*

FISH

You can buy fresh fillets of fish from fishmongers and supermarkets. Smoked fish has a stronger flavour than white fish. Ask an adult or the fishmonger to skin the fish for you.

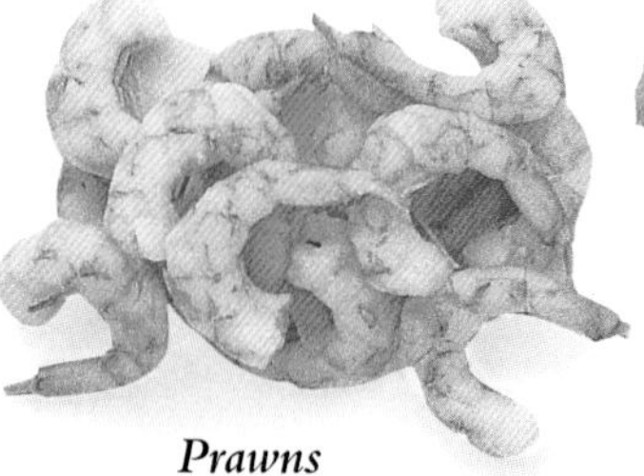

Prawns

Smoked haddock

Cod fillet

Prawns add a touch of luxury to a dish. You can add them to fish pie, savoury rice, or sauces. Make sure frozen prawns defrost thoroughly before using them.

MEAT

The most common types of red meat are pork, lamb, and beef. In general, the more expensive the meat is, the shorter the cooking time. Ask an adult to choose the right meat for you.

Minced beef

MINCED AND CUBED MEAT

Use minced beef to make hamburgers and Bolognese sauce for pasta. Buy meat already cut in cubes for the kebabs and casserole.

Pork

Beef

Lamb

CHICKEN

For making the spicy chicken, buy chicken cut into breast pieces and drumsticks. The best meat to use for kebabs is skinned chicken breast.

Chicken drumsticks

Chicken breast

Smoked streaky bacon

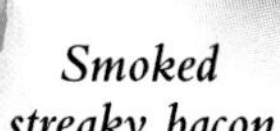

Frankfurter

SAUSAGES AND BACON

Streaky bacon is used to add flavour to a lot of dishes. There is a large range of sausages available. Try the different kinds and see which you like the best.

Pork chipolatas

Pork and garlic sausage

Pork and herb sausages

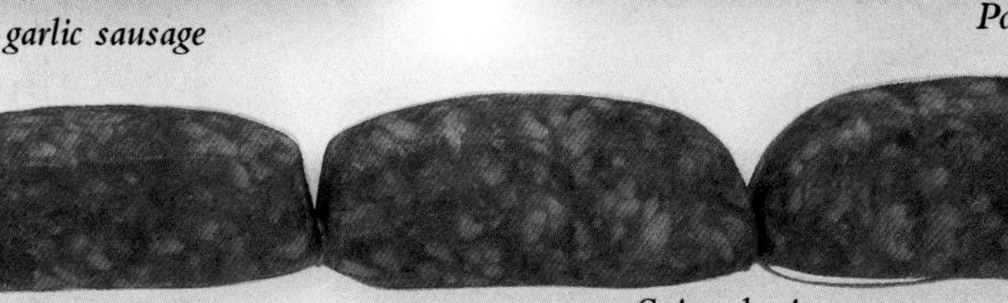

Spicy chorizo sausages

HAMBURGER FEAST

Home-made hamburgers taste far better than ready-made ones and they are really quick and easy to make. Why not experiment with lots of garnish ingredients and see whether you can invent a new king-sized hamburger?

COOK'S TOOLS

Mixing bowl • Chopping board
Fish slice • Sharp knife • Fork

You will need (for 4 servings)

For the burgers

1/2 an onion

1 egg yolk

450 g (1 lb) minced beef

1/2 teaspoon salt

1/2 teaspoon freshly ground black pepper

4 sesame seed hamburger buns

For the garnishes

Mayonnaise

Grilled rashers of bacon

Sliced cheese

Sliced tomatoes

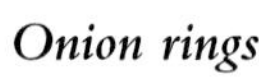

Onion rings

Lettuce leaves

What to do

1 Peel and finely *chop* the onion for the hamburgers. Slice the tomatoes and the onion rings for the garnishes.

2 Put the minced beef, egg yolk, chopped onion, salt, and pepper in the mixing bowl and mix them together well.

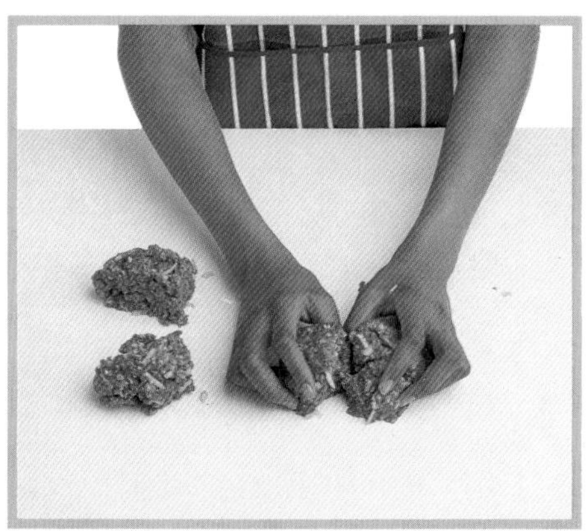

3 Split the hamburger mixture into four even-sized pieces and roll each one into a ball with the palm of your hand.

4 Then flatten each of the balls into a round hamburger. Firm the edges of the hamburgers to give them a good shape.

5 Heat the grill until hot, then *grill* the hamburgers on each side for 5 to 10 minutes, until firm and brown.

6 Put each hamburger in a roll. Then put sliced tomatoes, cheese, bacon, onion, or lettuce on top and add mayonnaise.

All in a burger

Arrange the garnishes carefully so they don't spill out of the burgers. Serve the burgers with tomato ketchup and relishes.

SALAD BURGER

BACON BURGER

KEBABS

Kebabs are grilled skewers of meat and vegetables. They are great for barbecues. Here you can see how to make sausage, chicken, and lamb kebabs as well as how to marinate, or soak, the meat in a sauce first to make it really tender.

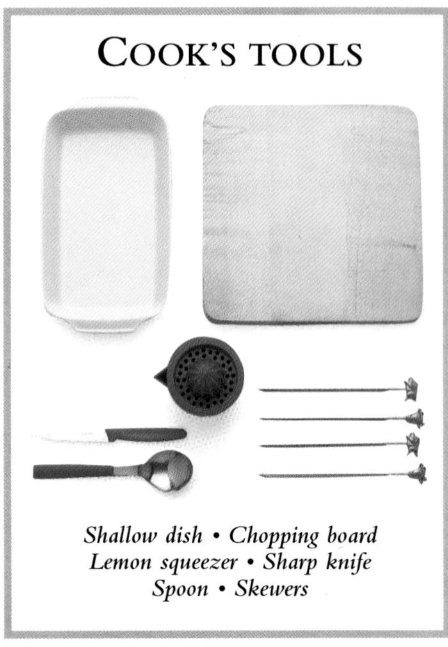

COOK'S TOOLS

Shallow dish • Chopping board
Lemon squeezer • Sharp knife
Spoon • Skewers

You will need (for 3 kebabs)

For the marinade

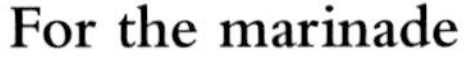

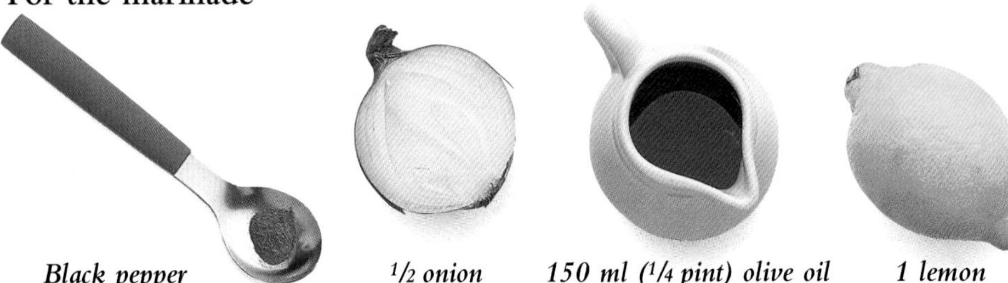

Black pepper · *1/2 onion* · *150 ml (1/4 pint) olive oil* · *1 lemon*

For the sausage kebab

For the chicken kebab

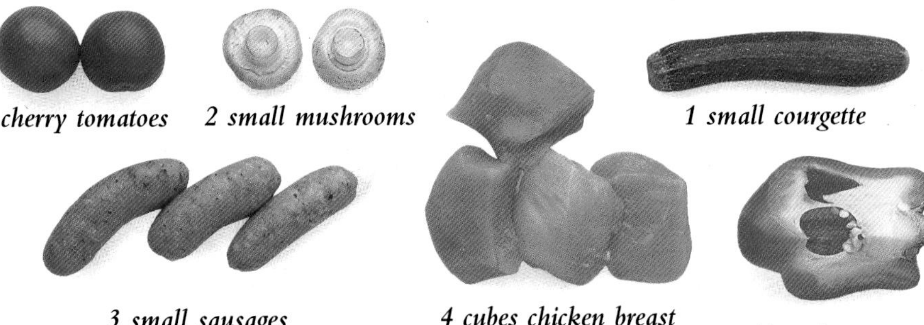

2 cherry tomatoes · *2 small mushrooms* · *3 small sausages* · *4 cubes chicken breast* · *1 small courgette* · *1/4 red pepper*

For the lamb kebab

1/4 green pepper

4 cubes lamb

2 small onions

2 dried apricots

Marinating meat

1 *Chop* the onion very finely. Cut the lemon in half and squeeze out the juice with the lemon squeezer.

2 Put the onion, the lemon juice, olive oil, and black pepper in the shallow dish and mix them together with a spoon.

3 Lay the cubes of meat in the mixture and leave them to *marinate* for a few hours, turning them now and then.

Making the kebabs

1 When you are ready to cook, prepare the vegetables. Cut the peppers into squares and the courgettes into short pieces.

2 Drain the meat, then push the chosen ingredients on to the skewers. Be careful of the sharp points on the skewers.

3 Preheat the grill, then *grill* the kebabs for about 10 minutes. Turn them once or twice so they cook all over.

A meal on a skewer

You can put together any ingredients you like for kebabs. Mix different meats and vegetables and choose colours as well as flavours that go well together.

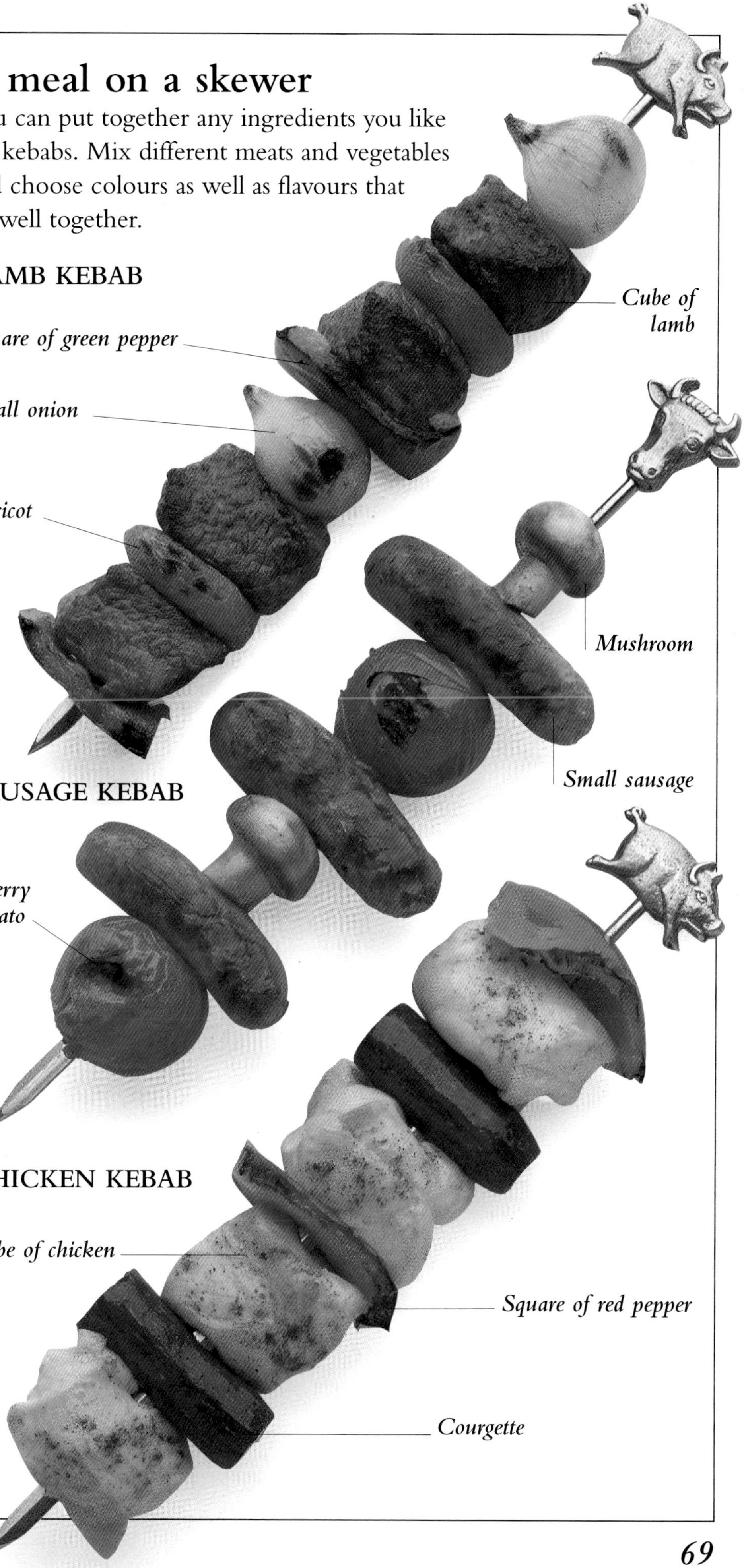

Lamb kebab

Square of green pepper

Small onion

Apricot

Cube of lamb

Sausage kebab

Cherry tomato

Mushroom

Small sausage

Chicken kebab

Cube of chicken

Square of red pepper

Courgette

SPICY CHICKEN

This wonderful recipe has a truly exotic flavour, created by a colourful mixture of spices. Allow a couple of hours to prepare the chicken, as it has to marinate (soak) in a spicy sauce for an hour before it is cooked, to make it tender.

COOK'S TOOLS

Large bowl • Chopping board
Sharp knife • Fork • Frying pan
Garlic press • Spoon
Wooden spoon • Baking sheet

You will need (for 4 servings)

4 chicken portions, each cut in half

225 g (8 oz) creamy yogurt

1½ tablespoons vegetable oil

1 large onion

1 clove garlic

Salt and pepper

1 teaspoon turmeric

1 teaspoon curry powder

¼ teaspoon cayenne pepper

What to do

1 Put the pieces of chicken on the chopping board and make two deep cuts across each of them with a sharp knife.

2 Mix half of the spices and a tablespoon of oil in the bowl. Add the chicken and turn it. Leave it to *marinate* for an hour.

3 Set the oven to 180°C/350°F Gas Mark 4. Put the chicken pieces on the baking sheet and *bake* them for 30 minutes.

4 *Chop* the onion. Heat the rest of the oil in the frying pan and fry the onion gently until soft and golden.

5 Mix the rest of the spices and crushed garlic into the yogurt until creamy. Add the fried onions and stir.

6 Spoon the mixture on top of the pieces of chicken. Then bake them for 20 to 30 more minutes until golden brown.

Eastern flavour

Serve the chicken on a bed of plain, cooked rice (see page 46) and garnish it with sprigs of fresh coriander.

Coriander

BEEF CASSEROLE

This rich casserole will really impress your family and friends, yet it doesn't take long to prepare. The secret of its success is that it has to be cooked slowly for quite a long time. This makes the meat very tender and gives the sauce a lot of flavour.

COOK'S TOOLS

Large plate • Chopping board Flameproof casserole dish • Garlic press Sharp knife • Wooden spoon Slotted spoon

You will need (for 4 servings)

2 onions

675 g (1½ lb) stewing or braising steak, cut into cubes

1 clove garlic

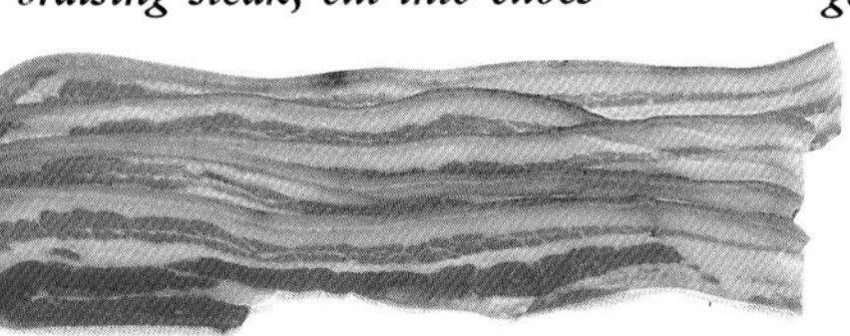

85 g (3 oz) streaky smoked bacon

450 ml (¾ pint) beef stock

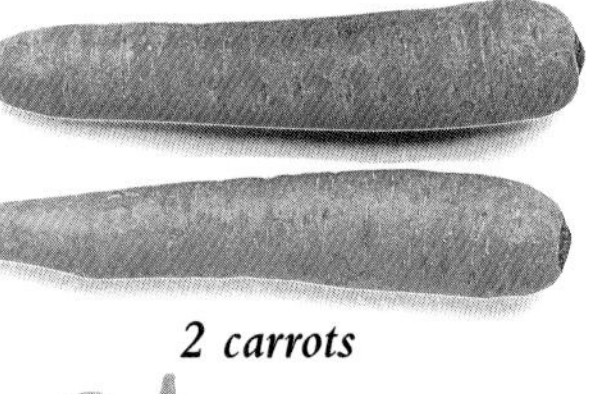

2 carrots

A few strips of orange peel

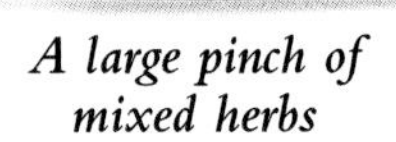

A large pinch of mixed herbs

2 tablespoons oil

2 tablespoons chopped parsley

1 tablespoon flour

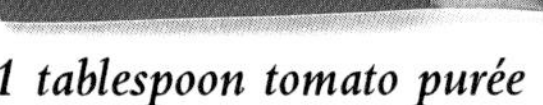

1 tablespoon tomato purée

Salt

Pepper

What to do

1 Set the oven to 180°C/ 350°F/Gas Mark 4. *Chop* the onions and bacon, slice the carrots, and *crush* the garlic.

2 Mix the flour, salt, and pepper on the plate. Lay the meat on top and turn it until each piece is coated in flour.

3 Heat a tablespoon of oil in the casserole and fry the carrots and onions for a few minutes. Remove with a slotted spoon.

4 Heat the rest of the oil in the casserole dish, then add the meat and stir it as it cooks until it is browned all over.

5 Return the vegetables to the casserole dish with the meat. Add the tomato purée, garlic, herbs, and orange peel and stir.

6 Add the stock and stir. Then put the lid on the casserole and cook it for about two hours until the meat is tender.

Meal in a pot

The finished casserole is rich and smooth. Sprinkle it with chopped parsley and serve it with baked, boiled, or mashed potatoes and a green vegetable.

Chopped parsley

FISHERMAN'S PIE

This is a warming dish which is good for cold days. It will also teach you two useful cook's skills: how to mash potatoes and how to make a white sauce. You can vary the recipe by using different types of fish, or by adding 115 g (4 oz) prawns.

COOK'S TOOLS

Baking dish • Chopping board
2 saucepans • Colander • Potato peeler
Sharp knife • Potato masher
Palette knife • Wooden spoon

You will need (for 4 servings)

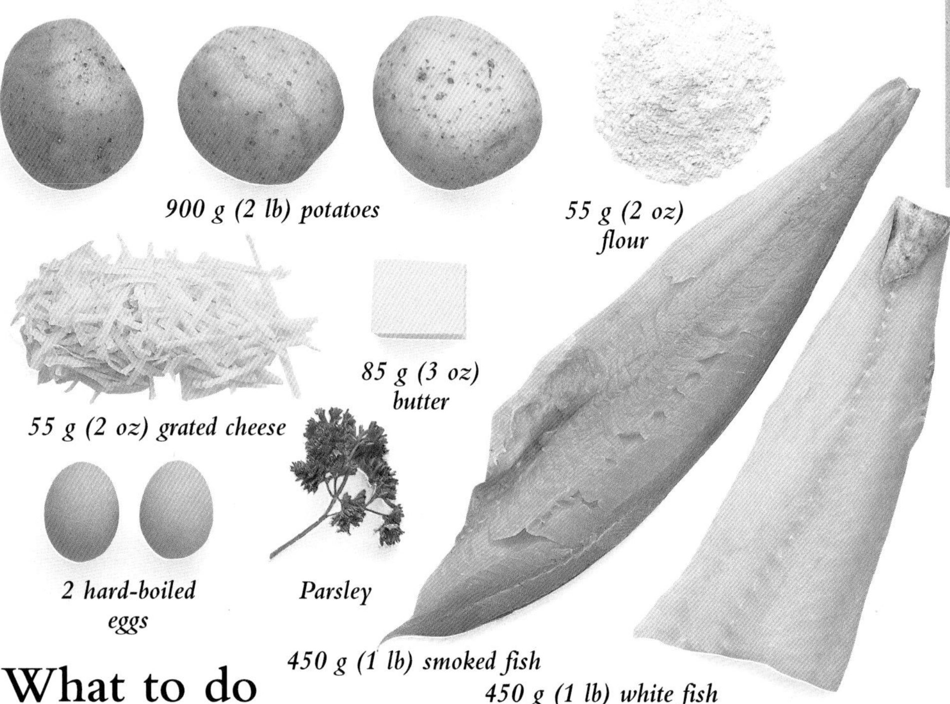

900 g (2 lb) potatoes

55 g (2 oz) flour

55 g (2 oz) grated cheese

85 g (3 oz) butter

2 hard-boiled eggs

Parsley

450 g (1 lb) smoked fish

450 g (1 lb) white fish

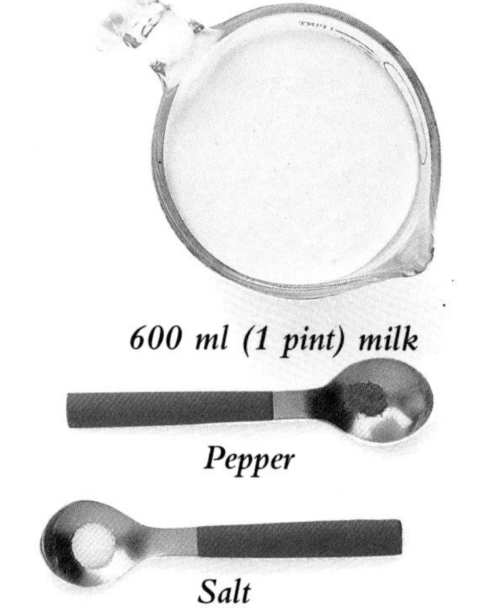

600 ml (1 pint) milk

Pepper

Salt

What to do

1 Set the oven to 200°C/ 400°F/Gas Mark 6. Peel the potatoes and put them in a saucepan of water to boil.

2 Meanwhile, cut the fish into chunks about 2½ cm (1 in) square. Chop the hard-boiled eggs and the parsley.

3 Then make a white sauce. Melt 55 g (2 oz) butter in a saucepan. Add the flour and stir it until it forms a thick paste.

4 Gradually stir the milk into the mixture. Cook over a low heat, stirring it as it thickens. Add parsley, salt, and pepper.

5 When the potatoes have cooked, drain them and mash them. Stir in the rest of the butter, a little milk, and salt and pepper.

6 Put the fish and chopped egg in the dish. Pour the sauce over them. Spoon the potato on top and sprinkle with cheese.

Hot from the oven

Bake the pie for about 30 minutes, until the potato topping is an even golden brown and crisp around the edges. Serve it with a green vegetable, such as broccoli or peas.

Parsley garnish

Potato topping

Parsley sauce

Fish

BISCUITS, BREAD, AND CAKES

Home baking is great fun. You can create all kinds of delicious treats, from gingerbread folk and fresh bread rolls to impressive iced cakes. This section of the book is full of basic recipes for biscuits, bread, and cakes which you can vary in different ways. Here are the main ingredients you will be using.

DRIED FRUIT

Dried fruits and glacé cherries are mainly added to cakes. Rinse the syrup off glacé cherries before using them.

Glacé cherries

Raisins

Apricots

Sultanas

Currants

SWEETENERS

Caster sugar is good for most cakes, biscuits, and meringues. Soft brown sugar and molasses sugar have a stronger taste and are good with wholewheat flour or in fruit cakes. Honey can also be used as a sweetener, where specified. Icing sugar, a very fine sugar, is used to make icing.

Soft brown sugar

YEAST AND BAKING POWDER

Yeast is added to bread and baking powder to cakes to make them rise when baked. The easiest yeast to use is quick-action dried yeast, which you just sprinkle on to the flour. Baking powder is added to plain flour for cakes.

Fresh yeast *Quick-action dried yeast* *Baking powder*

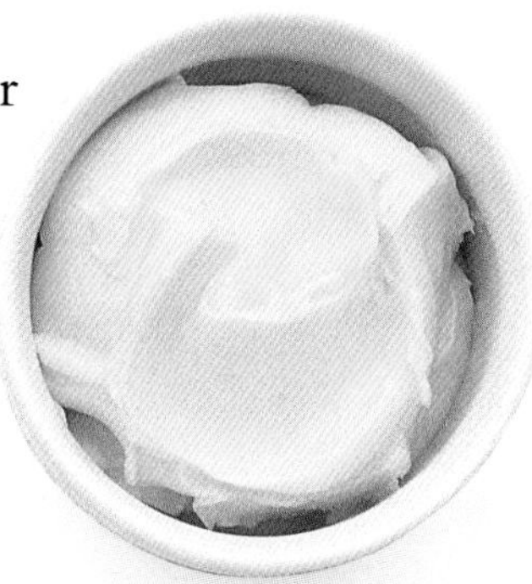

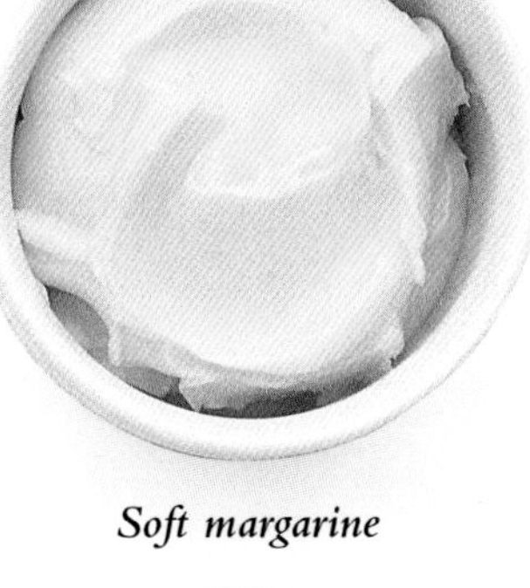

Soft margarine

Vegetable oil

FATS AND OILS

Butter has the best flavour for making cakes and biscuits, but margarine is also good. Soft margarine is used for all-in-one cake mixtures. Pastry is best made with a mixture of butter and lard or white vegetable fat. Vegetable oil is added to bread dough. Sunflower oil has a good mild flavour.

Butter

Lard or white vegetable fat

FLOUR

Plain white or wholemeal flour are best for cakes and pastries. If using white flour, look for unbleached flour. Use strong white flour for making bread. Self-raising flour has had baking powder added to it.

Unbleached, plain white flour

Plain white flour

Wholemeal flour

Honey

Caster sugar

Icing sugar

Molasses sugar

GINGERBREAD FOLK

You can cut these spicy gingerbread biscuits into people, trees, stars, and other shapes, then decorate them with icing. Here you can find out how to make the biscuits and over the page you can see how to ice them.

COOK'S TOOLS

*Baking trays • Rolling pin • Sieve
Wooden spoon • Pastry brush
Palette knife • Knife • Spoon
Fork • Biscuit cutters • Mixing bowl
Wire rack • Small bowl • Saucepan
Cocktail stick*

You will need (for about 30 biscuits)

340 g (12 oz) plain flour

115 g (4 oz) butter

2 teaspoons ground ginger

A few currants

1 teaspoon bicarbonate of soda

1 beaten egg

4 tablespoons golden syrup

175 g (6 oz) soft brown sugar

What to do

1 Set the oven to 190°C/ 375°F/Gas Mark 5. Melt some of the butter and *grease* the baking trays using a brush.

2 Put the butter, sugar, and syrup in a saucepan and stir them together over a low heat until they have melted.

3 *Sift* the flour, ground ginger, and bicarbonate of soda into the mixing bowl. Add the syrup mixture and the beaten egg.

4 Mix everything together, then *knead* it into a ball. Chill the dough in a plastic bag in the fridge for 30 minutes.

5 Sprinkle some flour on the table and rolling pin. Then *roll* the dough out until it is about 1/2 cm (1/4 in) thick.

6 Use the biscuit cutters, or a knife, to cut out the people and other shapes. Press the cutters down, then lift them off.

7 Lift the biscuits on to the baking tray. Then gather up the left-over dough, roll it out again and cut out more shapes.

8 Make holes with a cocktail stick in the top of any biscuits you want to hang up. Press currant eyes into the people.

9 *Bake* the biscuits for 10 to 15 minutes, until they are golden brown, then lift them on to a wire rack to cool.

ICING BISCUITS

We have piped white, green, and red icing on to the biscuits to decorate them. To make the leaf biscuits, mark the veins on with a knife while the biscuits are still uncooked. Let the other biscuits cool completely before icing them.

COOK'S TOOLS

3 teaspoons • Bowl
2 small bowls or cups
3 icing bags • Sieve

You will need (for 30 biscuits)

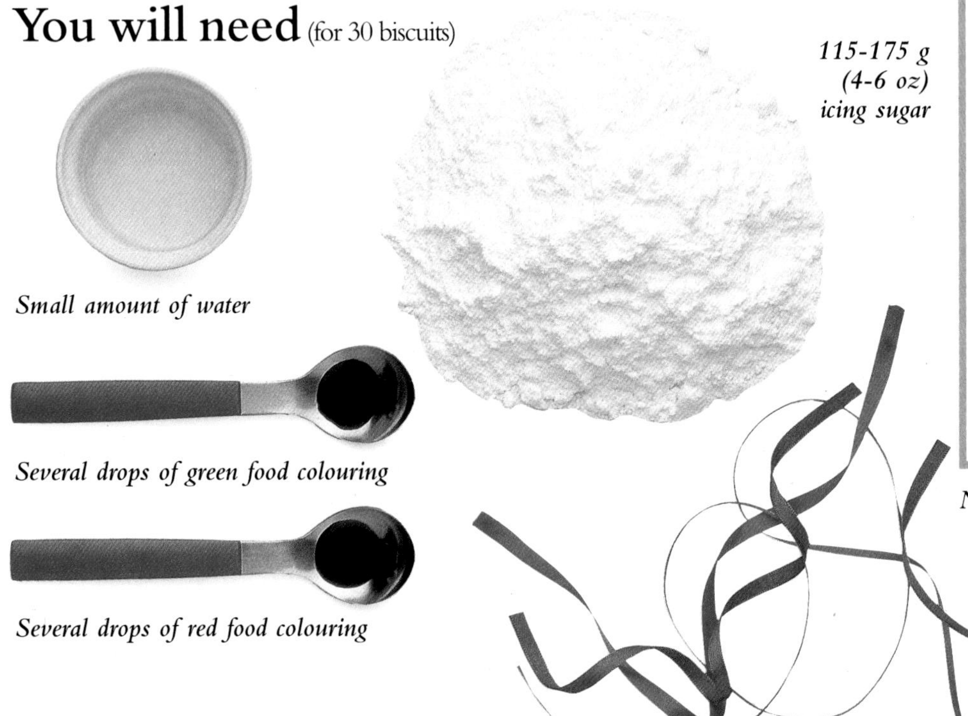

115-175 g (4-6 oz) icing sugar

Small amount of water

Several drops of green food colouring

Several drops of red food colouring

Narrow, coloured ribbons

What to do

1 *Sift* the icing sugar into the bowl. Add a little water at a time, mixing it into the sugar to make a thick, smooth paste.

2 Spoon a quarter of the icing into each of the two smaller bowls and add food colouring to it, to make green and red icing.

3 Fill the *icing bags* with the green, red, and white icing and pipe it carefully on to the biscuits, to make patterns.

Pretty as pictures

Why not try making a gingerbread family or your own Christmas tree decorations? Thread ribbon through the holes in the biscuits to tie them to the tree.

CHOCOLATE CHIP COOKIES

Here's a quick and easy recipe for some really traditional American cookies. The quantities given here will make about 18 cookies. You can vary them by adding 115 g (4 oz) of chopped walnuts if you like.

COOK'S TOOLS

Mixing bowl • Baking trays • Wire rack Wooden spoon • Teaspoon • Palette knife

You will need (for about 18 cookies)

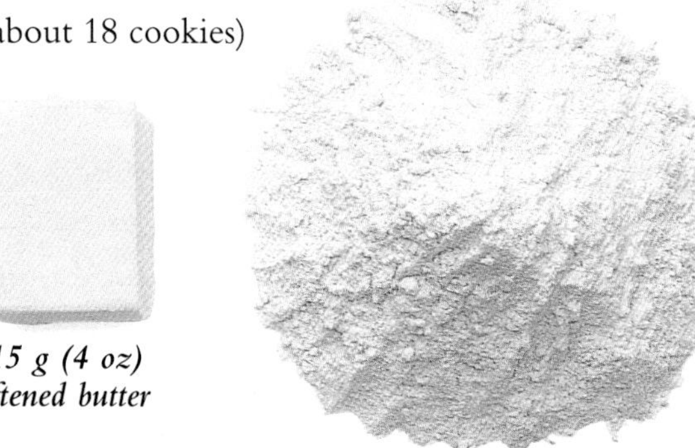

140 g (5 oz) plain flour

115 g (4 oz) softened butter

70 g (2½ oz) caster sugar

1 egg

½ teaspoon bicarbonate of soda

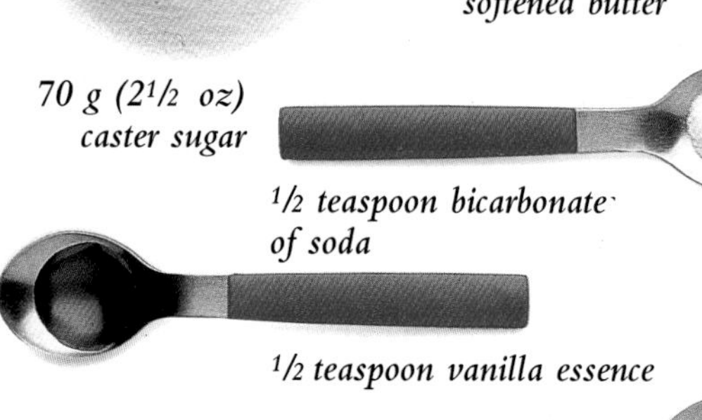

½ teaspoon vanilla essence

¼ teaspoon salt

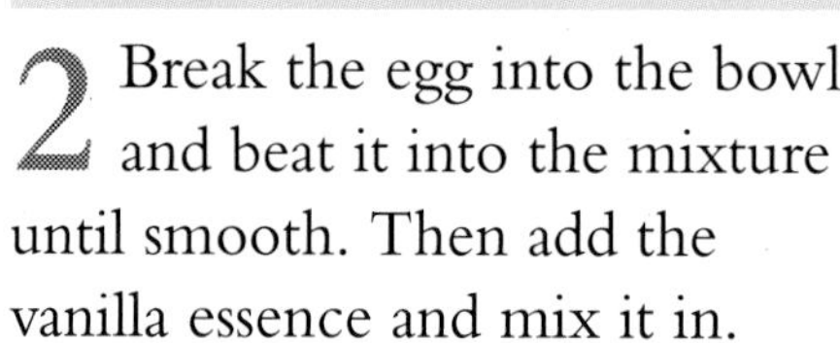

70 g (2½ oz) soft brown sugar

175 g (6 oz) chocolate chips

What to do

1 Set the oven to 190°C/375°F/Gas Mark 5. *Beat* the butter with both lots of sugar in a mixing bowl until creamy.

2 Break the egg into the bowl and beat it into the mixture until smooth. Then add the vanilla essence and mix it in.

3 Add the flour, salt, and bicarbonate of soda to the mixture, a little at a time, and stir everything together well.

4 Now add the chocolate chips and stir them in until they are evenly spread through the cookie mixture.

5 Butter the baking trays and spoon small mounds of the mixture on to them, leaving quite big spaces between the mounds.

6 *Bake* the cookies for 10 to 12 minutes until they are an even golden brown colour, then move them on to a wire rack to cool.

Chocolate chip cookies

Once the cookies are completely cool, store them in an airtight tin or container to keep them crisp and fresh.

The cookies should be crisp on the outside and slightly soft in the centre.

Chocolate chip

BAKING BREAD

There is something magical about making bread and watching it rise, yet it is very easy. This recipe will make a medium-sized plain or chocolate loaf and about eight rolls. Turn the page to see how to shape the rolls into lots of fun shapes.

You will need (for 1 loaf and 8 rolls)

1 dessertspoon sunflower oil

2 teaspoons salt

450 ml (3/4 pint) warm water

1 sachet (17 g or 1/2 oz) easy blend yeast

675 g (1 1/2 lbs) strong white or wholemeal flour

Sunflower seeds

Sesame seeds

For chocolate loaf

55 g (2 oz) sugar

55 g (2 oz) cocoa powder

COOK'S TOOLS

Mixing bowl • Tea towel
Sharp knife • 450 g (1 lb) loaf tin
Mini loaf tin • Wooden spoon
Pastry brush • Baking sheets
Measuring jug • Wire rack

What to do

1 Put flour, salt, and yeast (and sugar and cocoa powder if you are making the chocolate loaf) together in the bowl.

2 Add the sunflower oil and water and stir everything together with a wooden spoon until you have a soft *dough*.

3 Sprinkle some flour on the table. *Knead* the dough on it for about five minutes until it is smooth and elastic.

Loaf in a tin

Shape half the dough into a loaf and press it into an oiled tin. Cover with a tea towel and put it in a warm place for 40 minutes.

Shaping a round loaf

Roll half the dough into a ball and put it on a baking sheet. *Score* it with a knife, cover it with a tea towel, and let it rise.

Baking the loaf

Set the oven to 220°C/425°F/ Gas Mark 7. The loaf is risen when it has doubled in size. *Bake* the loaf for 35 minutes.

Warm from the oven

If the bread is not quite ready, bake it for a little longer. It is done when it sounds hollow if you tap it underneath. Once done, put it on a wire rack to cool. Bread is easier to slice when it is completely cold.

WHITE LOAF

Chocolate bread tastes savoury rather than sweet and is good with cheese. This loaf was shaped into a round and scored on top.

This classic white loaf was baked in a loaf tin. It has been decorated with pumpkin seeds. Seeds should be sprinkled on top of the loaf after it has risen, but before being put in the oven to bake.

CHOCOLATE LOAF

FUNNY ROLLS

Try making rolls with the rest of the bread dough. They will take about 20 minutes to rise. Brush them with milk if adding seeds. They are done when golden.

Shaping the rolls

Break the *dough* into about eight pieces of roughly the same size. Then roll them into small balls ready for shaping.

Flat bread

For a mini-loaf, shape one of the balls into a loaf and put it in an oiled tin. For a herb bread, flatten the balls into circles.

You will need

For herb bread topping

1 tablespoon sea salt

A sprig of rosemary

1 clove of garlic

Add oil, chopped garlic, rosemary, and salt on top before cooking.

1 tablespoon vegetable oil

For decorating mini-loaves

Currants

Sesame seeds

Poppy seeds

Cracked wheat

KNOT ROLL

Sesame seeds

HERB BREAD

MINI WHITE LOAF

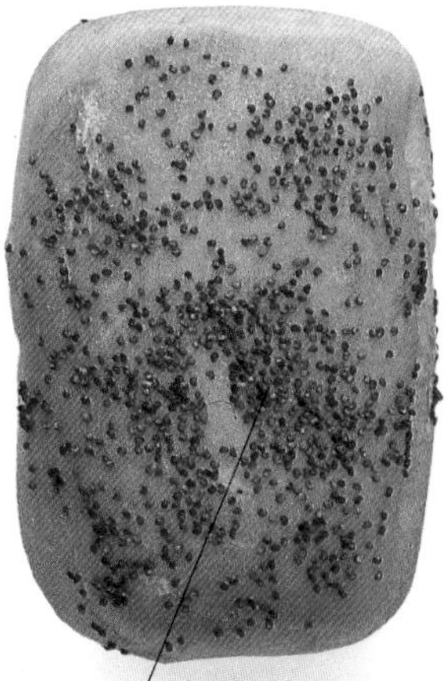

Poppy seeds

Rolling dough

To make knots, twists, and snails, start by rolling each ball of dough out into a long thin sausage shape with your hands.

Knots and twists

Fold the sausages into different shapes. Make a spiral for a snake or tie a sausage in a loose knot to make a knot roll. Let them rise.

Decorating

Preheat oven to 220°C/425°F/ Gas Mark 7. Decorate the rolls and lay them on an oiled baking sheet. Bake them for 15 minutes.

TWIST

Cracked wheat

SNAKE

Currant eyes

MINI MOUSE

Snip the dough to make ears

CROCODILE

Snip the dough to make crocodile scales

MINI CHOCOLATE LOAF

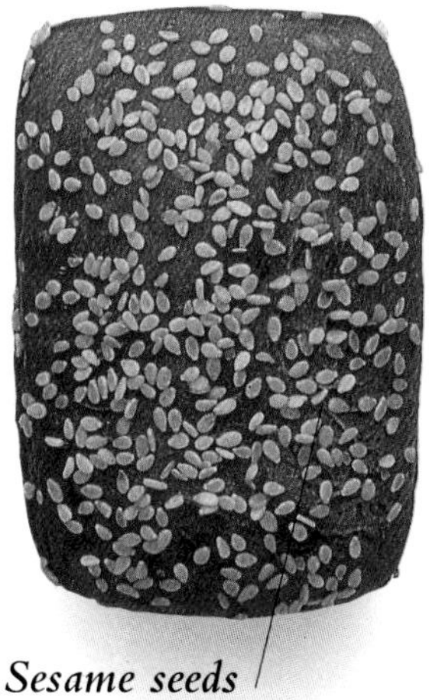

Sesame seeds

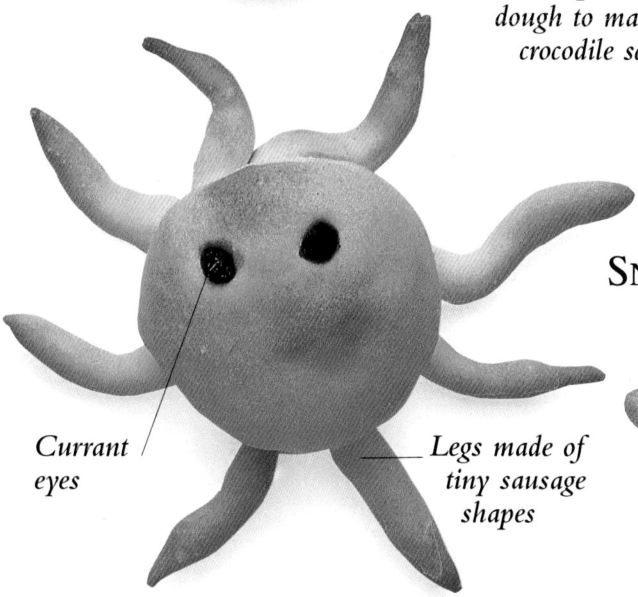

OCTOPUS

Currant eyes

Legs made of tiny sausage shapes

SNAIL

Small spiral stuck to body with water

Little Cakes

Why not make some little sponge cakes for tea? This recipe is for a basic sponge mixture which you can vary by adding cherries and coconut, or sultanas. The quantities will make 16 small cakes and 12 tiny ones. Turn the page for ideas on how to ice the cakes.

Cook's tools

Knife • Bun tins • Mixing bowl
Small bowl • Paper cake cases
and sweet cases • Wooden spoon
Big spoon • Teaspoon
Fork • Wire rack

You will need (for 28 cakes)

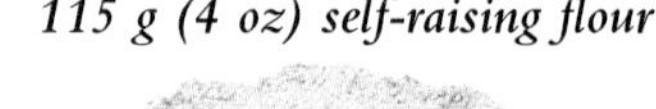

115 g (4 oz) caster sugar

2 medium-sized eggs

115 g (4 oz) self-raising flour

115 g (4 oz) softened butter

For sultana cake

115 g (4 oz) sultanas

For coconut cake

55 g (2 oz) desiccated coconut

115 g (4 oz) chopped glacé cherries

What to do

1 Set the oven to 190°C/ 375°F/Gas Mark 5. Put paper cake cases in one tin and paper sweet cases in the other.

2 Put the butter in the mixing bowl with the sugar. *Beat* the butter and sugar together until light and creamy.

3 Beat the eggs in a bowl with the fork. Add them to the butter mixture a little at a time using the wooden spoon.

4 Add the flour to the mixture a little at a time and *fold* it in gently. Add the sultanas or chopped cherries and coconut.

5 Spoon the cake mixture into the paper cases. *Bake* the tiny cakes for 10 minutes and the larger ones for 15 to 20 minutes.

6 The cakes are done when they are firm and golden brown. Take them out of the bun tins and move them to a wire rack to cool.

An array of cakes

The finished cakes are perfect for tea. Why not ice the plain ones for a special party? Turn the page to see what to do.

TINY CAKES

PLAIN CAKES

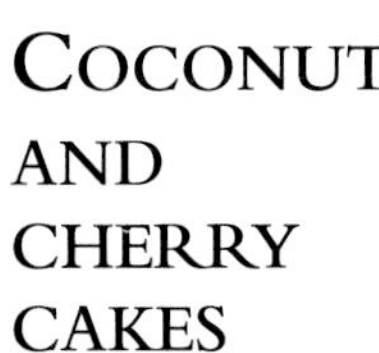

COCONUT AND CHERRY CAKES

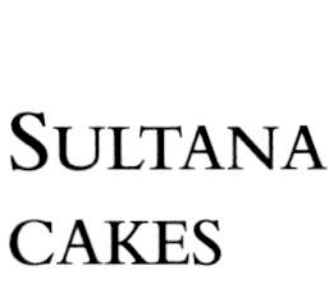

SULTANA CAKES

ICING LITTLE CAKES

For a special occasion it is fun to ice the cakes. Here we have used coloured icing with white piping. Mix the colouring into the icing a drop at a time until it is the right colour. You can find out how to make icing bags and do piping in the glossary (see page 126).

You will need (for about 30 cakes)

Blue food colouring

Yellow food colouring

Green food colouring

Red food colouring

Icing sugar

Water

Narrow, coloured ribbons

Candy-coated chocolate sweets

COOK'S TOOLS

Mixing bowl • Piping bag
4 small bowls • 4 teaspoons
Sieve • Wooden spoon

What to do

1 Make some icing (see page 80). Spoon a little icing into the four small bowls and stir a few drops of colouring into each one.

2 Put a little coloured icing on to each cake and spread it out evenly to the edges of the cake with the back of a teaspoon.

3 Let the coloured icing dry, then fill the *piping bag* with white icing and *pipe* patterns on top of the cakes.

Balloons away!

Why not ice the bigger cakes to look like balloons? Tuck ribbons beneath them to look like swirling strings. Decorate the tiny cakes with sweets in contrasting colours.

Lines piped in white icing

Candy-coated chocolate sweet

ICED SPONGE CAKE

This cake is very easy to make as all the ingredients are mixed together in the same bowl. You can flavour it with orange, lemon, or chocolate. Use chocolate icing for the filling in the middle and the coating on top. Turn the page for tips on decoration.

You will need (for one cake)

115 g (4 oz) softened margarine

2 large eggs

115 g (4 oz) caster sugar

115 g (4 oz) self-raising flour

2-3 drops vanilla essence

A pinch of salt

1 teaspoon baking powder

COOK'S TOOLS

Wire rack • 2 circles greaseproof paper 17.5 cm (7 in) across • 2 x 17.5 cm (7 in) sandwich cake tins • Mixing bowl Pastry brush • Wooden spoon Palette knife

For icing the cakes

Bowl • Saucepan • Wooden spoon

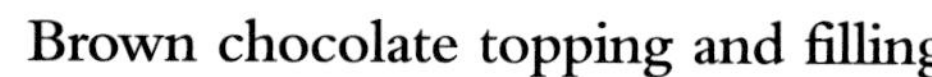

For lemon cake

Grated rind of a lemon
1 tablespoon lemon juice

For orange cake

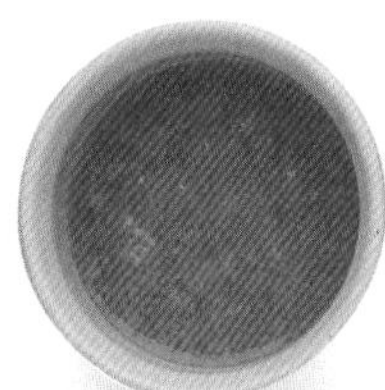

Grated rind of an orange
1 tablespoon orange juice

For chocolate cake

30 g (1 oz) sieved cocoa powder, to replace same amount of flour

Brown chocolate topping and filling

115 g (4 oz) milk chocolate

2 tablespoons soured cream

White chocolate topping and filling

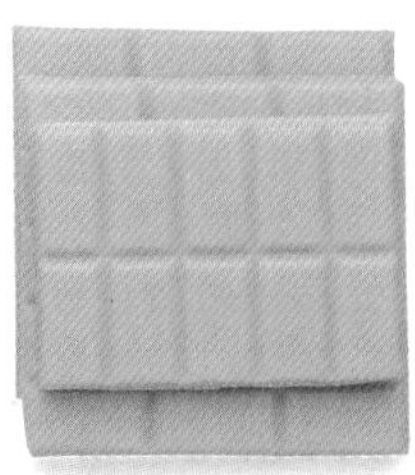

175 g (6 oz) white chocolate

2 tablespoons soured cream

What to do

1 Set the oven to 170°C/ 325°F/Gas Mark 3. Put all the ingredients for the cake you are making in the mixing bowl.

2 Mix all the ingredients together with the wooden spoon, then *beat* the mixture hard for about two minutes.

3 The cake mixture should drop off a spoon easily. If it seems too stiff, stir in two teaspoons of water and beat it again.

4 Divide the mixture between two *greased* and *lined* cake tins and smooth it level. *Bake* the cakes for 30 minutes until firm.

5 Slide a knife around the edges of the tins to loosen them and turn them out on to a wire rack. Remove the wax paper.

Icing the cakes

1 Break the chocolate up into a small bowl. Pour in the soured cream. Heat a saucepan of water over a low heat.

2 Stand the bowl over the saucepan of water. Stir the chocolate and cream together until the chocolate has melted.

3 When the cakes are cool, turn one of them upside down and spread half of the chocolate icing on it with a palette knife.

4 Put the other cake on top of the icing, then spread the rest of the icing smoothly on top of the sandwich cake.

CAKE DECORATING

The best part of making a cake is decorating it! Wait for the icing to set, then gather your decorations together and work out how to arrange them on a large plate. If you haven't got the exact ingredients shown here, you can use similar nuts, sweets, or fruit. Try out ideas of your own.

You will need (for 4 cakes)

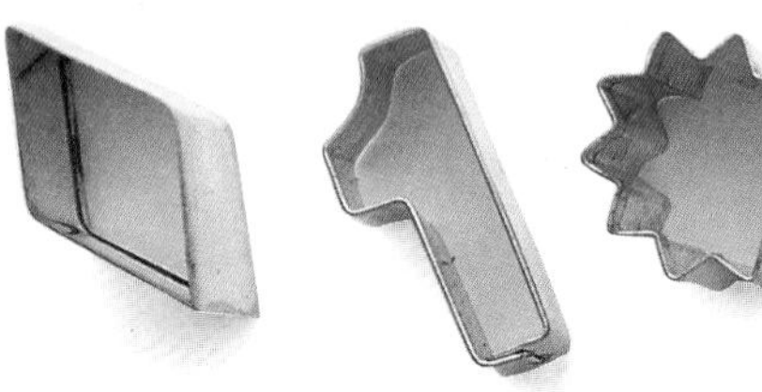

Cutters for making different shapes

Red licorice strings (or use red piped icing)

White fondant icing or marzipan

Red fondant icing or marzipan

Split almonds

Hundreds and thousands

White chocolate drops

Dark chocolate drops

Glacé cherries

Candy-coated chocolate sweets

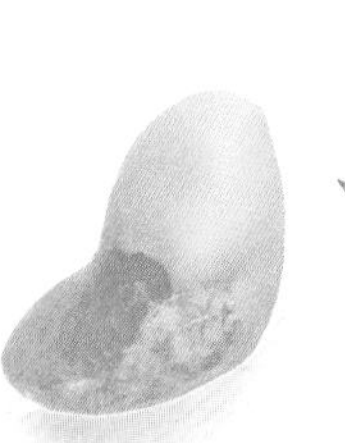

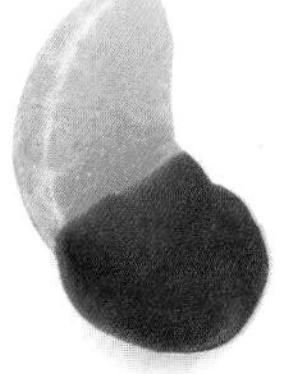

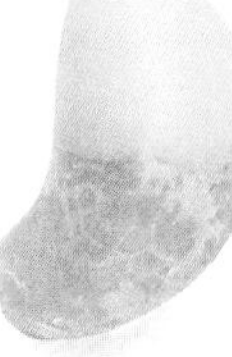
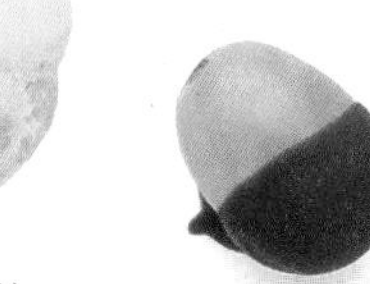

Chocolate-dipped fruit *(see page 101)*

FLOWER CAKE

White chocolate drops

Split almonds

FUNNY FACE

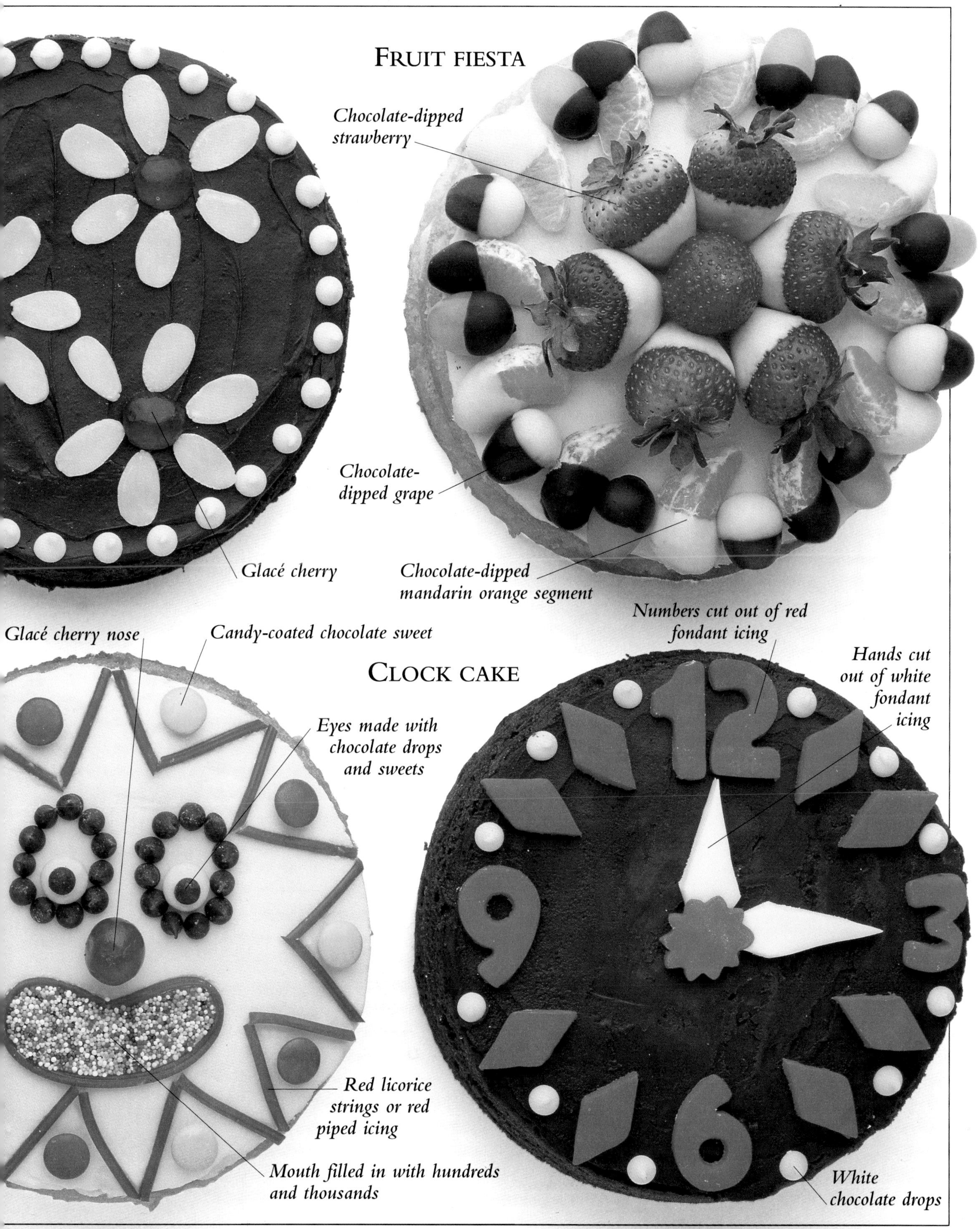
FRUIT FIESTA
Chocolate-dipped strawberry
Chocolate-dipped grape
Glacé cherry
Chocolate-dipped mandarin orange segment
Glacé cherry nose
Candy-coated chocolate sweet
CLOCK CAKE
Numbers cut out of red fondant icing
Hands cut out of white fondant icing
Eyes made with chocolate drops and sweets
Red licorice strings or red piped icing
Mouth filled in with hundreds and thousands
White chocolate drops

PUDDINGS AND TREATS

The puddings in this part of the book are based on fruit and chocolate and range from scrumptious chocolate-dipped fruit to hot apple pie. While making them you can also learn useful basic skills, such as how to make pastry, meringues, and pancake batter. Here is a quick guide to the key ingredients.

NUTS

Nuts go really well with both fruit and chocolate. You will find them in the baking section of a supermarket. For extra flavour and crunchiness, toast them under the grill (ask an adult to help).

Hazelnuts

Walnuts

Blanched (skinned) almonds

CHOCOLATE

Look for chocolate with a high percentage of cocoa solids (check the package). More expensive types of chocolate taste better and melt more easily.

Chocolate buttons

Chocolate drops

Milk chocolate

White chocolate

Dark chocolate

FRUIT

Choose fresh fruit for puddings whenever possible. Fruit should be a good colour, firm, and not have any marks on it. Otherwise use fruit that has been canned in natural fruit juices. Frozen soft fruit is also good. Allow it to defrost before using it.

CREAM AND YOGURT

Use double cream or whipping cream for whipping. Single cream is better for pouring. Greek-style yogurt is thick and creamy. Bio yogurt contains less fat and has a good, mild flavour.

ICE-CREAM SAUCES

You can make ice-cream even more scrumptious by serving it with different-flavoured sauces. Here are three quick and easy sauces which can transform an ordinary pudding into something really special.

COOK'S TOOLS

Sieve • Bowl • Blender
Tin opener • Whisk • Wooden spoon
Cherry stoner • Saucepan

You will need (for 4 servings)

For chocolate sauce

115 g (4 oz) plain chocolate

150 ml (1/4 pint) water

150 ml (1/4 pint) double cream

2 teaspoons caster sugar

For raspberry sauce

2 tablespoons double cream

4 tablespoons icing sugar

225 g (8 oz) frozen raspberries

For hot cherry sauce

400 g (15 oz) tin of cherries in syrup

2 teaspoons cornflour

Hot cherry sauce

1 Stand the sieve over the bowl and pour the opened tin of cherries into it so that the syrup drains into the bowl beneath.

2 Pour the syrup into the saucepan, then *stone* the cherries and put them in the saucepan with the syrup.

3 Mix the cornflour into a paste with some of the syrup, then stir it into the pan and gently heat the sauce until it thickens.

Chocolate sauce

1 Break the chocolate into pieces into the saucepan, then add the double cream, the sugar, and the water.

2 Heat the mixture until it *simmers* and the chocolate melts. Let it simmer for five minutes, *whisking* all the time.

Raspberry sauce

Put the thawed raspberries, sugar, and cream in the blender and whizz it for about 30 seconds until everything is mixed together.

All on a sundae

Try the sauces out with different ice-creams to find out which combinations you like best. Mix raspberry with chocolate, or hot cherry with strawberry.

CHERRY DREAM

Hot cherry sauce

Strawberry ice-cream

BANANA SPLIT

Chocolate sauce

Banana cut in half lengthways

Vanilla ice-cream

RASPBERRY VELVET

Raspberry sauce

Raspberries for decoration

Chocolate ice-cream

CHOCOLATE TREATS

Try these delicious nibbles – mini-florentines and chocolate-dipped fruit. You will need to allow at least one hour for the chocolate to set when making them. A 115 g (4 oz) bar of chocolate will make eight mini-florentines.

COOK'S TOOLS

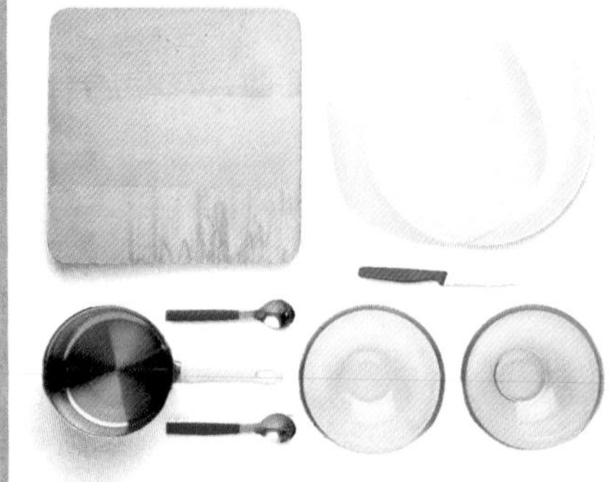

Chopping board • Plate • Circle of non-stick silicone paper • Sharp knife Saucepan • 2 teaspoons • 2 bowls

You will need (for 4 servings)

Good quality white chocolate

Good quality milk chocolate

Mixed nuts

Glacé cherries

Sultanas or raisins

Dried apricots

White grapes

Strawberries

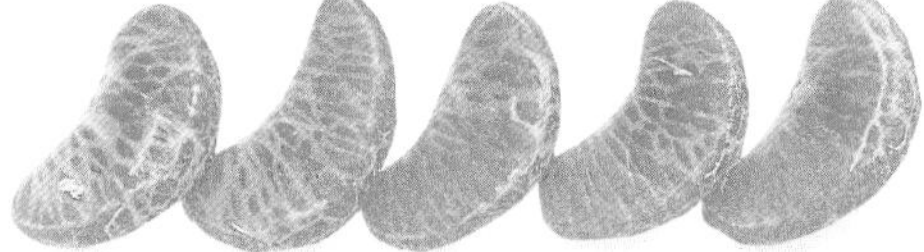

Tangerine segments

Mini-florentines

1 Break the chocolate up into the two bowls. Put the white chocolate in one bowl and the milk chocolate in the other.

2 Heat water in a saucepan and stand each bowl in it in turn over a low heat. Stir the chocolate until it has melted.

3 Put the silicone paper on the plate and drop teaspoons of brown and white melted chocolate on to it.

Chocolate dips

4 Chop the cherries and dried apricots, then arrange the fruit and nuts on the chocolate and put it in a cool place to set.

1 Dip strawberries, grapes, and tangerine segments halfway into the melted chocolate, then lay them on the silicone paper.

2 Put the treats in a cool place for one to two hours until the chocolate has set hard. Then peel them gently off the paper.

Tasty treats

Arrange the mini-florentines and chocolate-dipped fruits in a pretty pattern on a plate. Store the treats in a cool place, but not in the fridge.

Mini-florentine

Chocolate-dipped tangerine segment

Chocolate-dipped strawberry

Chocolate-dipped grape

BISCUIT CAKE

This scrumptious cross between a cake and a giant biscuit can be eaten as a pudding or as a wicked tea-time treat. The clever thing about it is that you don't have to cook it in the oven but just put it in the fridge until it sets hard.

COOK'S TOOLS

Chopping board • Mixing bowl
20 cm (8 in) cake tin
Aluminium foil • Saucepan
Sharp knife • Wooden spoon

You will need (for 1 cake)

115 g (4 oz) plain chocolate

2 tablespoons double cream

55 g (2 oz) glacé cherries

225 g (8 oz) digestive biscuits (or any other plain biscuits)

115 g (4 oz) butter

55 g (2 oz) flaked almonds

30 g (1 oz) raisins

What to do

1 Line the cake tin with a large piece of foil. Press the foil carefully into the tin, being careful not to tear it.

2 Chop the cherries. Put the biscuits in the mixing bowl and break them up into small pieces. Add the cherries.

3 Break the chocolate into the saucepan. Add the butter and cream and stir over a low heat until the chocolate has melted.

4 Add the raisins and almonds to the biscuit mixture, then pour in the chocolate sauce. Stir everything together well.

5 Spoon the mixture into the cake tin and press the cherries on top. Cover the cake with foil and press it down firmly.

6 Put the cake in the fridge for about two hours until it has set hard. Then lift it out of the tin and peel off the foil.

The finished cake

This cake is so rich that it is best to cut it into small pieces. It should be big enough for eight to ten pieces. People can always have second helpings – if there is any left...

Glacé cherry

Raisin

Flaked almond

FRUIT FRISBEES

You can make mouth-watering fruit tarts really easily by using ready-made puff pastry. The secret is to slice the fruit thinly and to arrange it attractively. The quantities below will make three frisbees and two banana boomerangs.

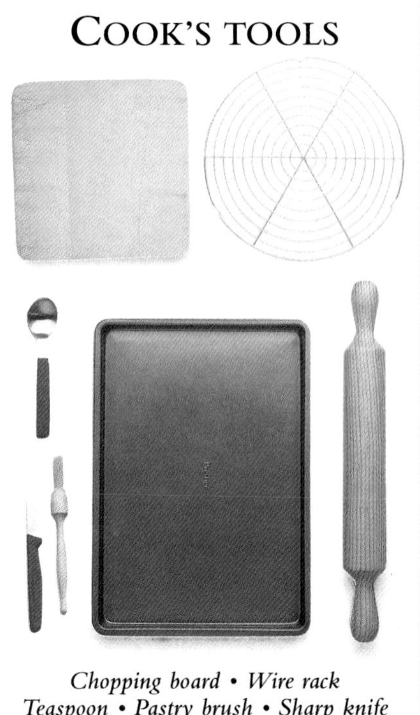

COOK'S TOOLS

Chopping board • Wire rack
Teaspoon • Pastry brush • Sharp knife
Baking tray • Rolling pin

You will need (for 5 tarts)

225 g (8 oz) ready-made puff pastry

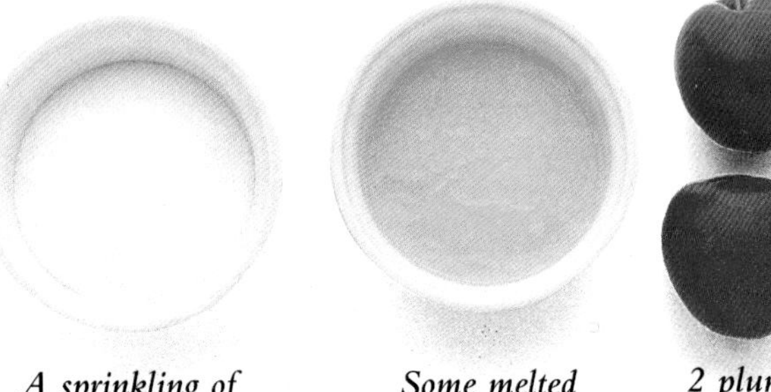

A sprinkling of caster sugar

Some melted butter

2 plums

Warmed, sieved apricot jam

A pear

Sliced peaches

A glacé cherry

A banana

What to do

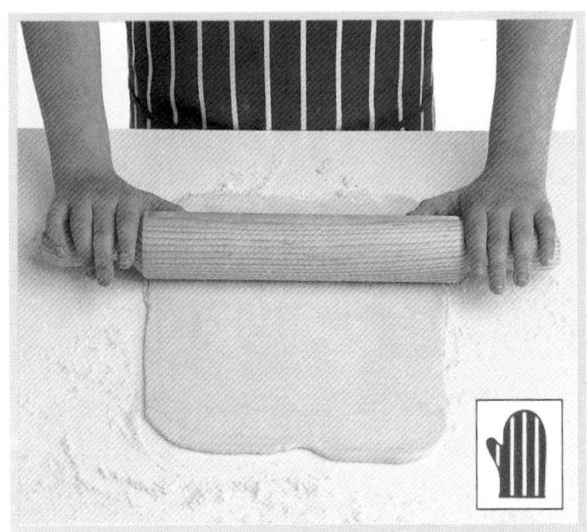

1 Set the oven to 220°C/ 425°F/Gas Mark 7. *Roll out* the pastry on a floured surface until about 3 mm (1/8 in) thick.

2 Cut circles out of the pastry around a dish or lid. Then cut around a banana twice to make two banana shapes.

3 Slice the plums and pear. Then brush the pastry with the melted butter and arrange slices of fruit on the circles.

4 Cut the banana in half and lay it on the pastry bananas. Brush the prepared fruit with butter and sprinkle sugar on top.

5 *Bake* the tarts for 20 minutes, until the pastry is crisp and the fruit cooked. Put them on a wire rack to cool.

6 When the tarts have cooled, brush the fruit with a little melted, sieved apricot jam, to *glaze* the tarts.

Frisbees and boomerangs

These crisp tarts make scrumptious puddings. Serve them on their own or with a dollop of cream.

Glacé cherry, added before glazing, for decoration

BANANA BOOMERANG

Glazed half of a banana

PEACH FRISBEE

PEAR FRISBEE

Sliced peaches

Thinly sliced pears, arranged in a fan

PLUM FRISBEE

FRUIT IN THE OVEN

Baked apples and bananas are wonderful cold weather puddings and they are one of the easiest things to prepare. Add a little butter, sugar, and a sprinkling of sultanas and just bake them in the oven until they are deliciously soft.

COOK'S TOOLS

Ovenproof baking dish
Chopping board • Lemon squeezer
Bowl • Grater • Apple corer
Teaspoon • Sharp knife

You will need (for 6 servings)

For baked bananas

2 bananas

1 tablespoon brown sugar

15 g (1/2 oz) butter

Half an orange

1 tablespoon sultanas

For baked apples

2 tablespoons clear honey

2 tablespoons water

4 big dessert apples

55 g (2 oz) sultanas or raisins

A pinch of cinnamon

30 g (1 oz) butter

30 g (1 oz) brown sugar

Baked apples

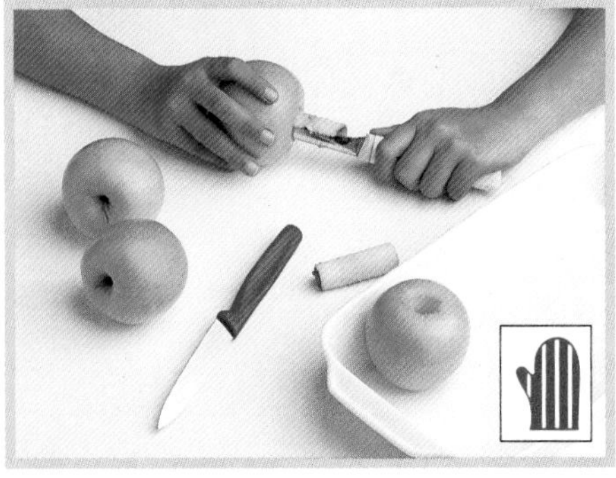

1 Set the oven to 190°C/ 375°F/Gas Mark 5. Make a cut around the middle of each apple and then *core* it.

2 Mix the sultanas, sugar, and cinnamon together in a bowl, then spoon the mixture into the hole in each apple.

3 Put a knob of butter on each apple and pour the honey and water on top. *Bake* the apples for 40 minutes, or until soft.

Baked bananas

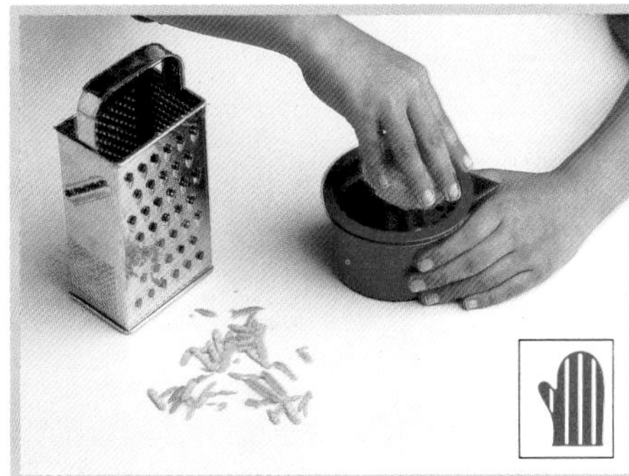

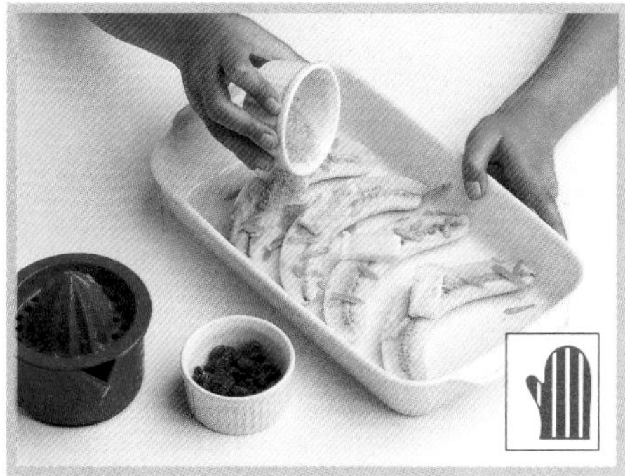

1 Set the oven to 220°C/425°F/Gas Mark 7. *Grate* the rind of the orange, then squeeze out the juice. *Grease* the dish.

2 Peel the bananas, cut them in half lengthways and lay them in the dish. Sprinkle them with orange rind and juice.

3 Put a knob of butter on each banana and sprinkle sugar and sultanas on top. Bake them for 10 to 12 minutes, until soft.

Hot from the oven

You can eat the apples and bananas on their own or serve them with fresh cream or custard (see pages 110 and 113).

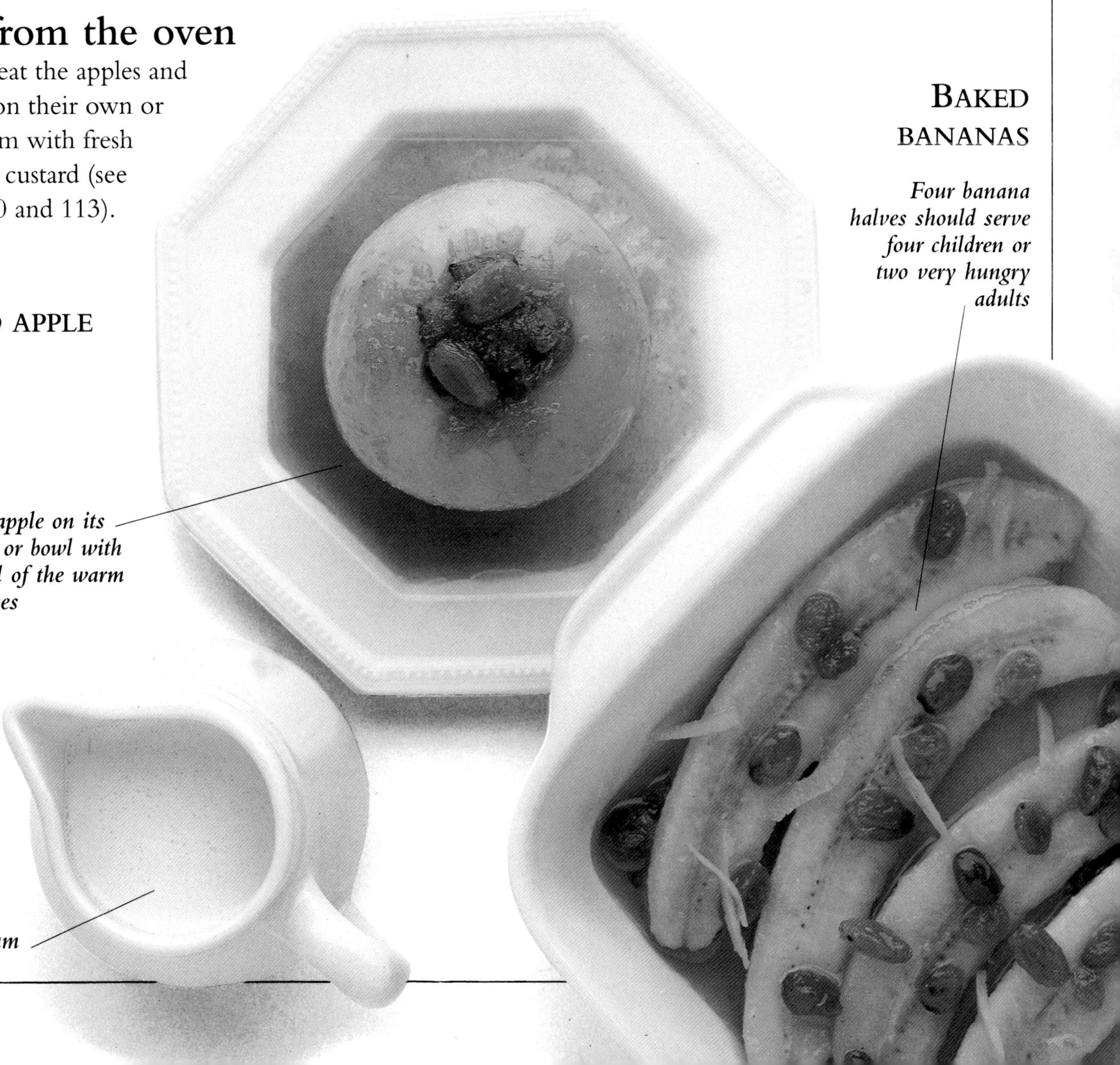

BAKED APPLE

Put each apple on its own plate or bowl with a spoonful of the warm honey juices

BAKED BANANAS

Four banana halves should serve four children or two very hungry adults

Fresh cream

FRUIT BASKETS

These delicious desserts are meringue baskets filled with fresh cream and topped with fruit. The secret of good meringue is to cook it at a low temperature until it is really dry. So allow a couple of hours for cooking to make it really perfect.

COOK'S TOOLS

Baking sheet • Non-stick baking parchment • Mixing bowl • Wire rack Chopping board • Sharp knife Teaspoon • Small bowl • Whisk

You will need (for 6 meringues)

A pinch of salt

2 egg whites

115 g (4 oz) caster sugar

A sprig of mint

Any fruit you like

Black and white grapes

Raspberries

Strawberries

Sliced peaches

Tinned mandarin oranges

Pineapple chunks

150 ml (1/4 pint) double cream or whipping cream

What to do

1 Set the oven to 120°C/ 250°F/Gas Mark 1/2. *Line* the baking tray with a piece of non-stick baking parchment.

2 Pour the egg whites into the mixing bowl. Add the salt and *whisk* them together until the egg whites form stiff peaks.

3 Add the caster sugar, a little at a time, and keep whisking until all the sugar has been mixed into the egg whites.

4 Spoon small mounds onto the baking sheet, making a dip in centre of each one. *Bake* for about two hours until they are dry.

5 Whisk the cream until it is thick. Pick the stalks off the strawberries and cut all the fruit into slices or small pieces.

6 Spoon whipped cream into the meringue nests, then arrange the sliced fruit on top, to look like flower petals.

CARNATION

Pineapple chunk

Sliced strawberry

ROSE

Raspberry

POPPY

Green grape

Strawberry half

PANSY

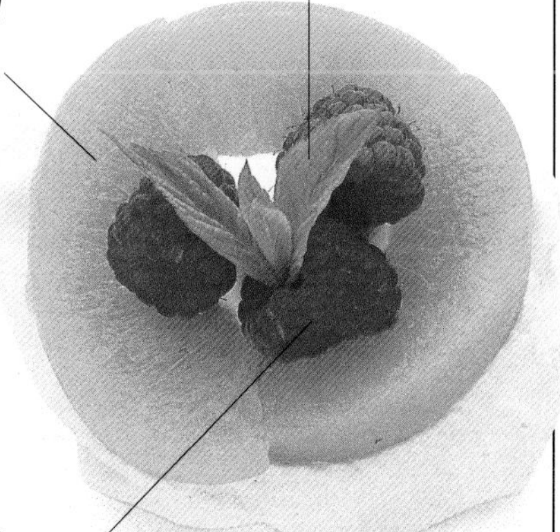

Mint leaves

Sliced peach

Raspberry

ORCHID

Black grape

Tinned mandarin orange

NARCISSUS

Half a slice of peach

Raspberry

APPLE PIE AND CUSTARD

Here you can find out how to make a fruit pie. You can make it with apples or any other fruit you like – the choice is yours! Turn the page to see how to decorate the pie and make a yummy custard to pour over the top.

COOK'S TOOLS

For the pie

Mixing bowl • Chopping board
Rolling pin • Skewer • Pastry brush
Small star-shaped cutter • Pie dish
Bowl • Potato peeler • Large spoon
Sharp knife

For the custard

Saucepan
Wooden spoon • Bowl

You will need

(for 1 pie and custard)

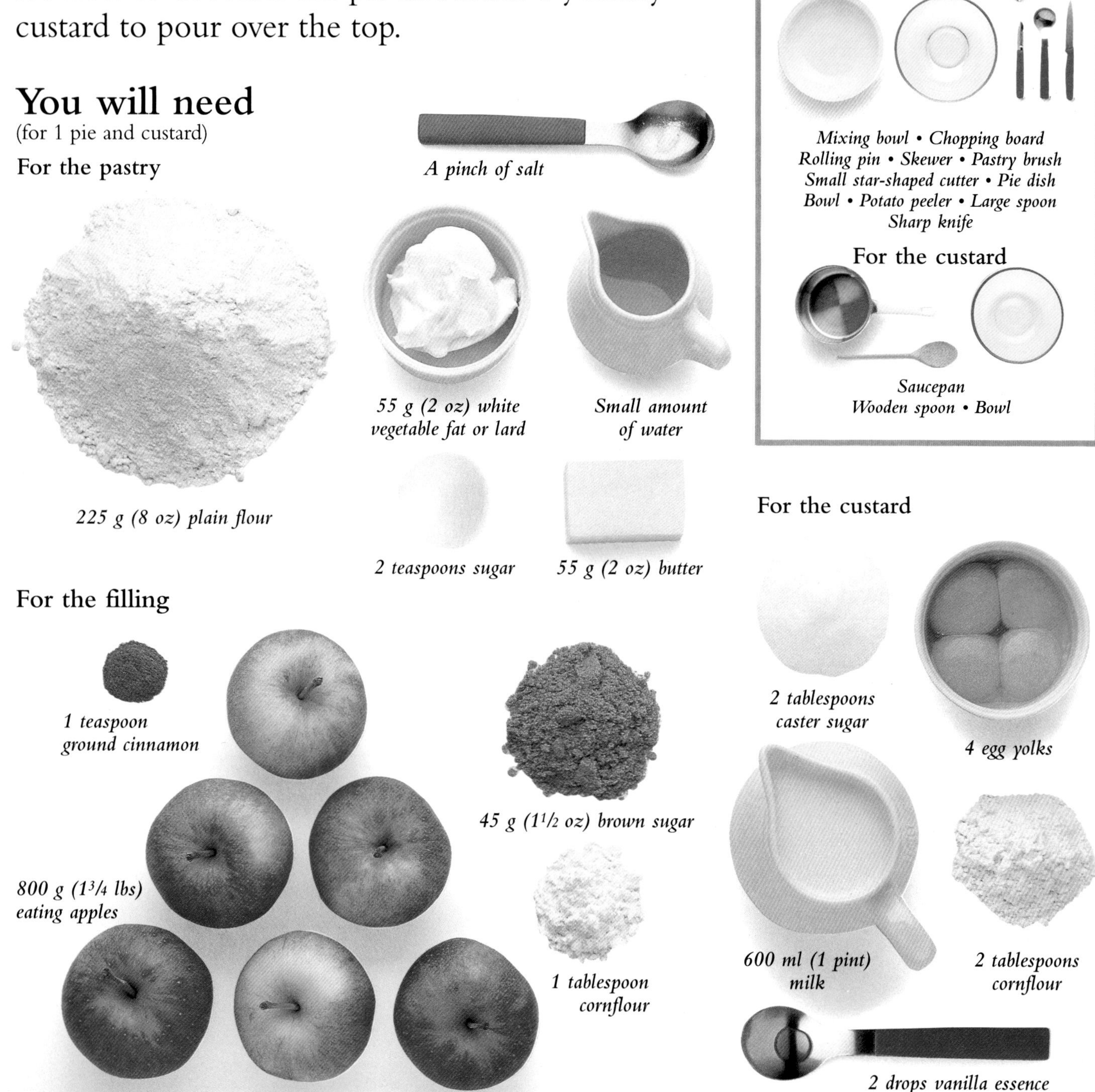

For the pastry

A pinch of salt

225 g (8 oz) plain flour

55 g (2 oz) white vegetable fat or lard

Small amount of water

2 teaspoons sugar

55 g (2 oz) butter

For the filling

1 teaspoon ground cinnamon

800 g ($1\frac{3}{4}$ lbs) eating apples

45 g ($1\frac{1}{2}$ oz) brown sugar

1 tablespoon cornflour

For the custard

2 tablespoons caster sugar

4 egg yolks

600 ml (1 pint) milk

2 tablespoons cornflour

2 drops vanilla essence

Making the pie

1 Set the oven to 200°C/ 400°F/Gas Mark 6. *Rub* the flour, butter, and white fat together in the mixing bowl.

2 When the mixture is like fine breadcrumbs, add the sugar, then add about 3 tablespoons water and mix it in well.

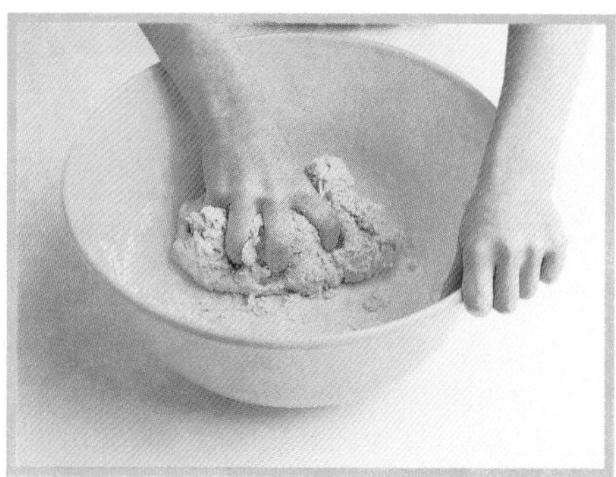

3 Gently *knead* the mixture into a ball of *dough*. If the dough seems too crumbly, add a little more water.

4 Peel the apples and cut them into quarters. Cut out the cores and pips, then cut each apple quarter in half.

5 Put the sliced apples in a bowl. Add the brown sugar, cornflour, and cinnamon and mix everything together.

6 Sprinkle flour on the table and *roll out* three-quarters of the pastry into a circle 1/2 cm (1/4 in) thick and bigger than the dish.

7 Lay the pie dish on top of the pastry and cut round it. Then cut a strip of pastry to go round the edge of the dish.

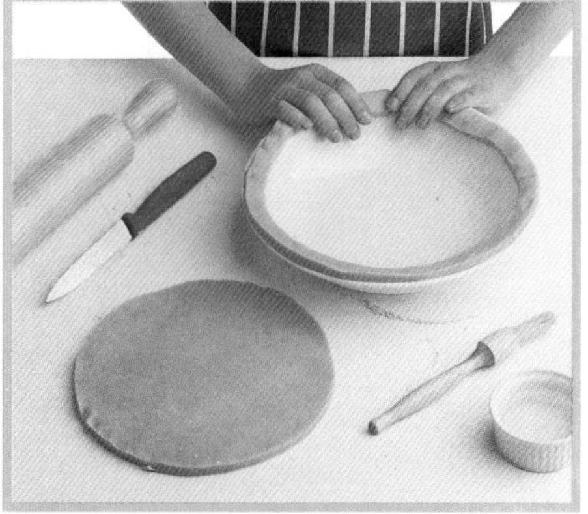

8 Press the pastry strip round the dish and brush it with water. Put the apples in the dish and lay the pastry on top.

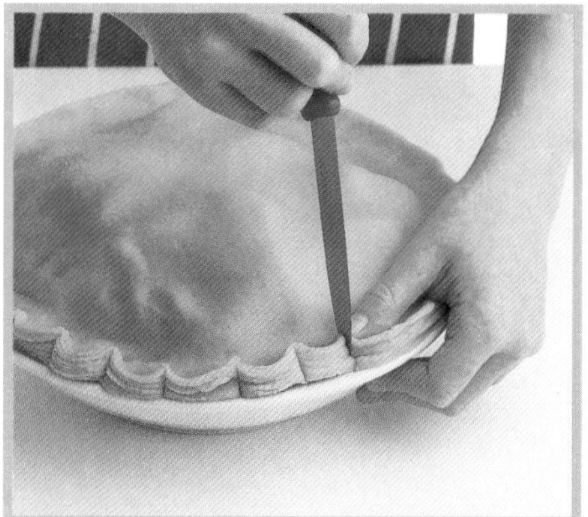

9 Press the edges of the pastry together and trim them. Then make a pattern round them with a knife, as shown.

DECORATING THE PIE

1 Roll out the pastry you have left. Cut two-thirds of it into narrow strips and cut small stars out of the rest with a cutter.

2 Brush the pastry with water. Make a cross with two long strips and stripes with the rest. Prick air holes with the skewer.

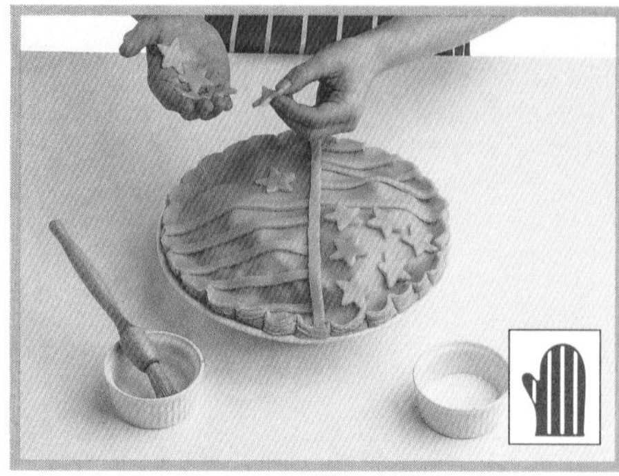

3 Lay stars on the rest of the pastry, then sprinkle it with sugar. *Bake* the pie for 45 minutes until golden brown.

Other decorations

We have used stars and stripes to make an all-American apple pie, but you can decorate a pie with any shapes you like. Choose a theme, or just use the cutters you have at home.

LOVING HEARTS

LEAFY APPLES

GRACEFUL FLOWER

Hot from the oven

Serve the apple pie hot, along with a jug of home-made custard to pour on top. Or try it with thick, whipped cream.

Making the custard

1 Heat the milk in a saucepan over a medium heat until it starts to look frothy on top. Take the pan off the heat.

2 Mix the egg yolks, sugar, vanilla essence, and cornflour together in a bowl. Then stir in the hot milk, a little at a time.

3 Pour the mixture back into the saucepan and cook it over a low heat. Stir it until it has thickened to a creamy sauce.

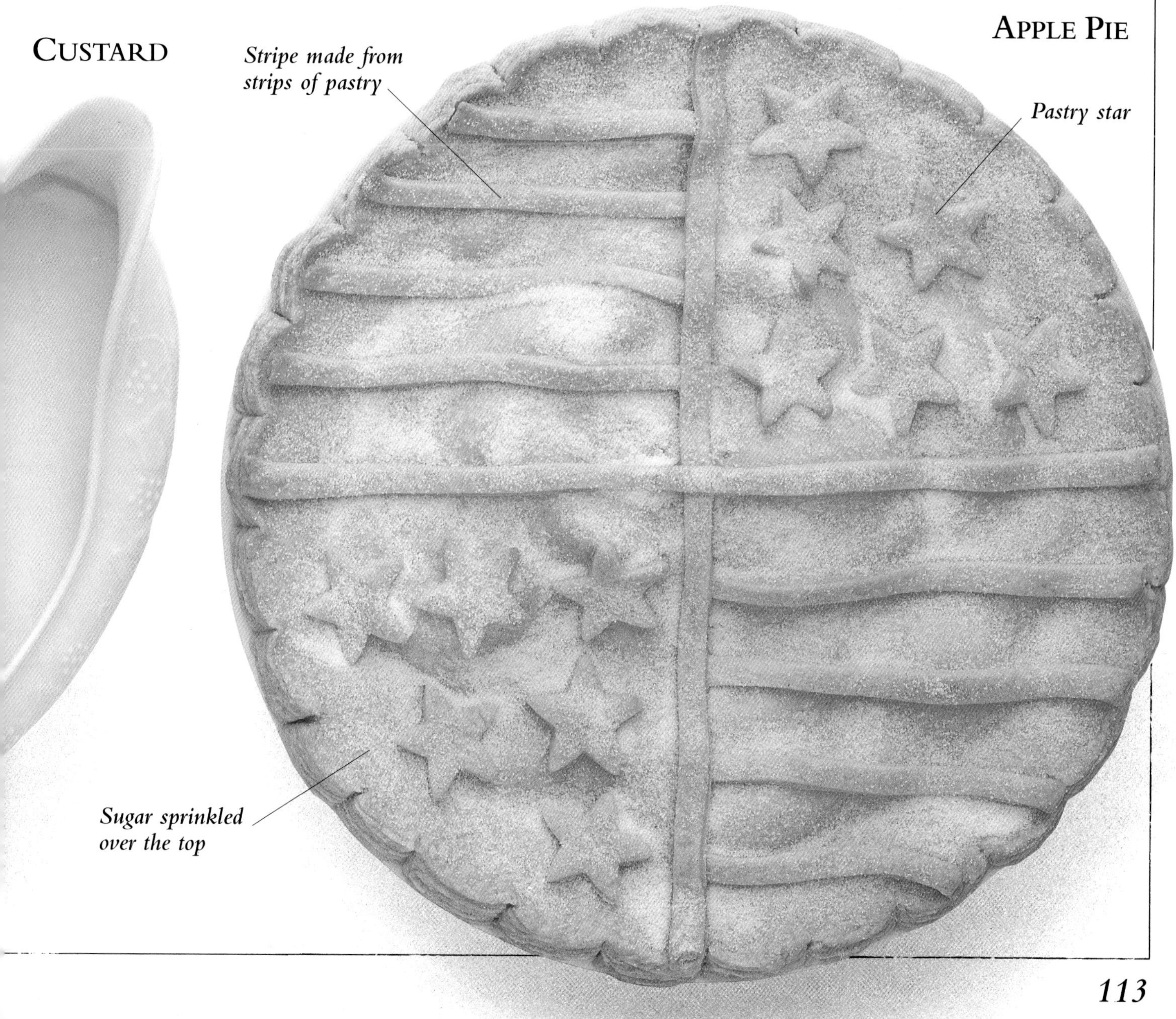

CUSTARD

APPLE PIE

Stripe made from strips of pastry

Pastry star

Sugar sprinkled over the top

PANCAKE TIME

Make these foolproof pancakes and fill them with whatever you like. With practice you should get 12 thin pancakes out of the amounts given here. Stack the pancakes on a warm plate as you make them and fill them when you are ready to eat.

COOK'S TOOLS

Bowl • Plate • Fish slice • Whisk
17.5 cm (7 in) frying pan
Pastry brush • Spoon • Measuring jug

You will need (for 12 pancakes)

A pinch of salt

2 eggs

115 g (4 oz) plain flour

4 tablespoons melted butter

300 ml (1/2 pint) milk and water mixed together

What to do

1 Put the flour and salt in a bowl. Add the eggs and some of the milk and water, and *whisk* in the flour, a little at a time.

2 Then gradually pour the remaining milk and water into the mixture, whisking it until the ingredients are well mixed in.

3 Add half the melted butter to the mixture and whisk it again. This smooth, creamy mixture is called the *batter.*

4 Brush the frying pan with a little melted butter and heat it until it sizzles. Then pour in two tablespoonfuls of batter.

5 Quickly tilt the pan from side to side until there is a thin layer of batter spreading across the base of the frying pan.

6 Cook the pancake for about a minute, then flip it over, cook it for 10 more seconds and slide it onto a warm plate.

Hot pancakes

When you are ready to eat, spread the pancakes with filling and roll or fold them in any of the ways shown here.

FANS

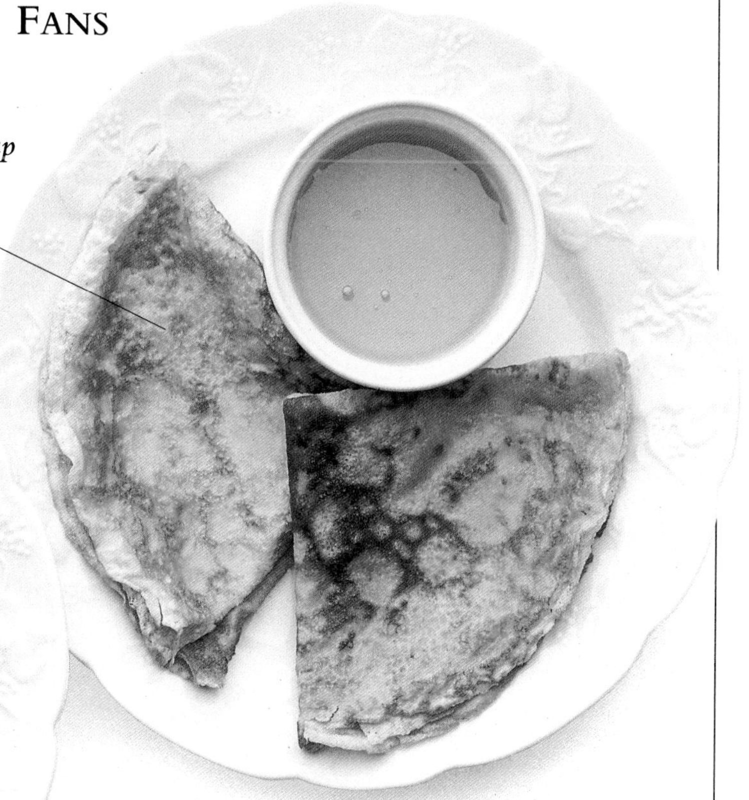

Try spreading the pancakes with syrup and folding them into triangles.

JAM PARCELS

These pancakes were spread with jam and folded into squares.

LEMON ROLLS

Or sprinkle your pancakes with lemon juice and sugar and simply roll them up.

PICNIC TIME

Why not put together a picnic using recipes from the book? Wrap things in aluminium foil, arrange home-made bread rolls in baskets, and put salad in containers.

FILLED ROLLS
(pages 20-21)

GREEK SALAD
(pages 56-57)

TARTS
(pages 36-39)

FRESH BREAD ROLLS
(pages 84-87)

CHOCOLATE MILKSHAKE
(pages 24-25)

FRUIT FRISBEES
(pages 104-105)

CHOCOLATE BISCUIT CAKE
(pages 102-103)

PARTY TIME

Choose the most colourful recipes from the book for your party. Start with savoury snacks, then move on to sweet things and finish with a special birthday cake.

SNACKS ON STICKS
(pages 14-15)

FINGER BITES
(pages 18-19)

MINI-PIZZA
(pages 50-51)

ICE-CREAM SUNDAES
(pages 98-99)

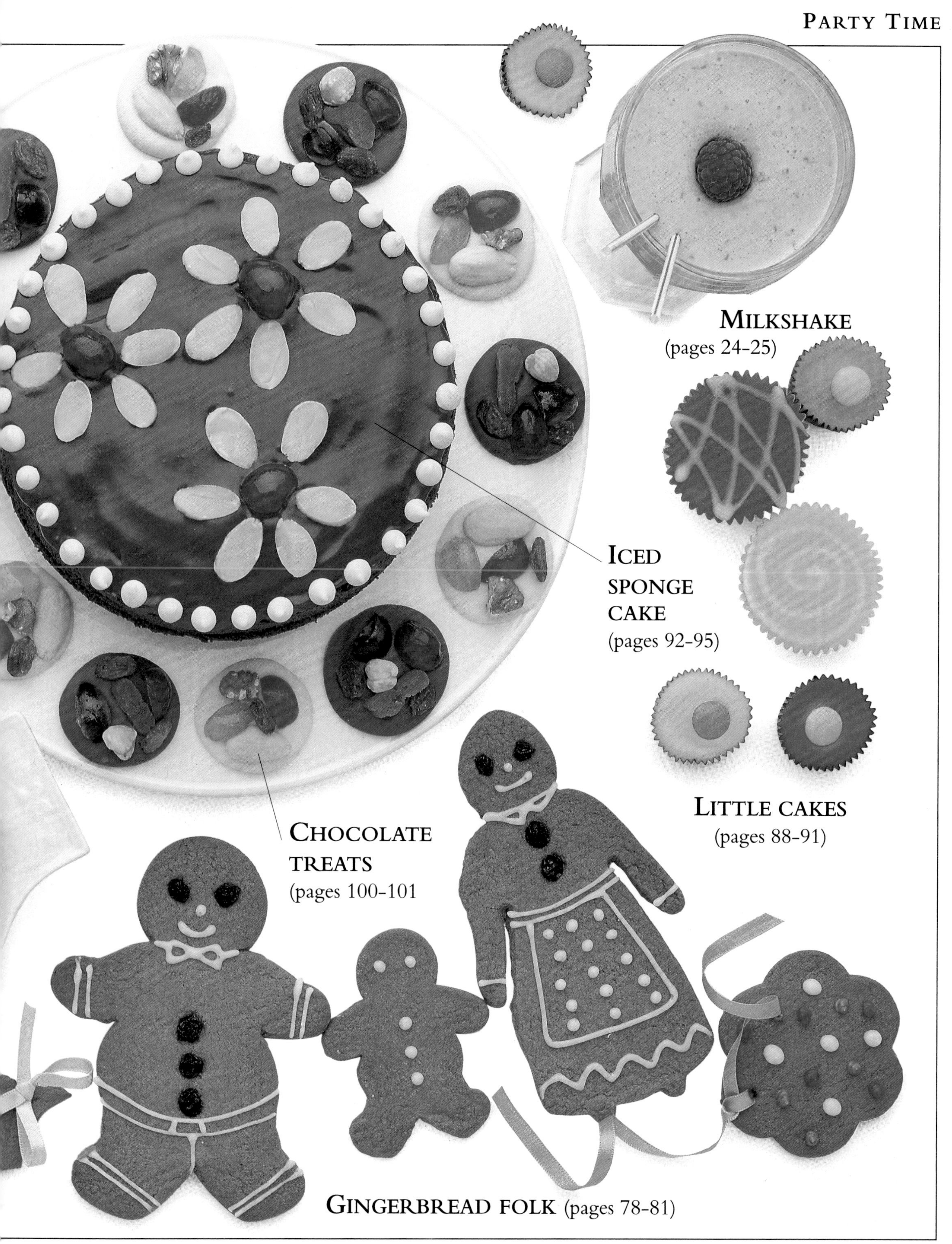
MILKSHAKE
(pages 24-25)
ICED SPONGE CAKE
(pages 92-95)
LITTLE CAKES
(pages 88-91)
CHOCOLATE TREATS
(pages 100-101
GINGERBREAD FOLK (pages 78-81)

MENU PLANNER

Here are some ideas for meals you can put together from recipes in this book. When you are planning a meal, try to choose things with contrasting flavours, colours, and textures. Choose the main course first, then plan the rest of the meal around it.

A PIZZA FEAST

Mini-pizzas *(pages 50-51)*

Fruit kebabs *(pages 14-15)*

A SUMMERY MEAL

Greek salad *(pages 56-57)*

Fresh bread rolls *(pages 84-87)*

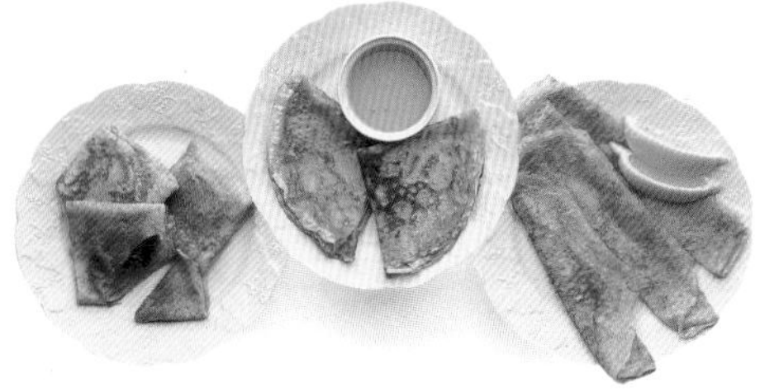

Pancakes *(pages 114-115)*

ITALIAN-STYLE LUNCH

Creamy spaghetti *(pages 42-43)*

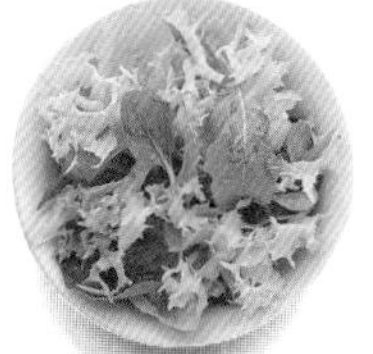

Green salad *(pages 56-57)*

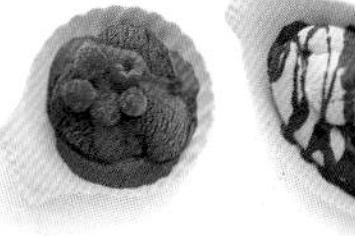

Ice-cream sundaes *(pages 98-99)*

VEGETARIAN MEAL

Vegetables and rice *(pages 46-47)*

Fruit frisbees *(pages 104-105)*

WINTER WARMER

Beef casserole *(pages 72-73)*

Boiled potatoes and broccoli *(pages 54-55)*

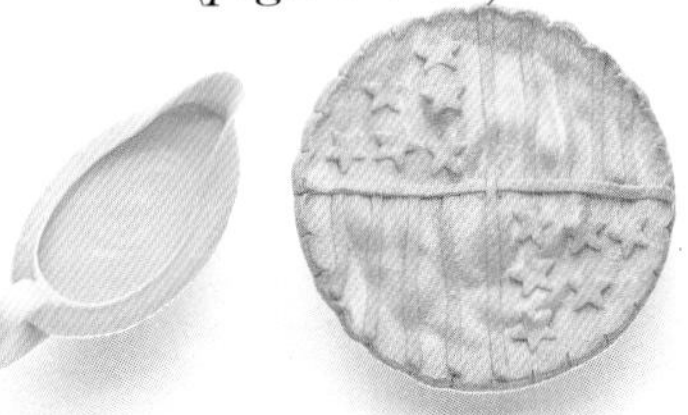

Apple pie and custard *(pages 110-113)*

EXOTIC LUNCH

Spicy chicken *(pages 70-71)*
Boiled rice *(page 46)*

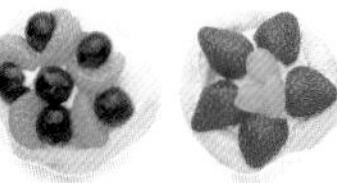

Fruit baskets *(pages 108-109)*

FAST FOOD

Hamburgers *(pages 66-67)*

Milkshakes *(pages 24-25)*

PICTURE GLOSSARY

This is a picture guide to some of the special terms that cooks use most often. Here you can find out what each term means and learn, step-by-step, how to master the most useful basic cookery skills.

Slicing

To slice vegetables, hold them firmly on a chopping board and slice downwards. Hold the knife against your knuckles, as shown, so you do not cut your fingers.

Chopping herbs

To chop fresh herbs, such as parsley, bunch the stalks together and hold them down on the board while you slice the leaves finely.

Shredding a lettuce

Hold the lettuce down on a board and cut across it in very fine slices. This will give you thin ribbons of lettuce.

Dicing

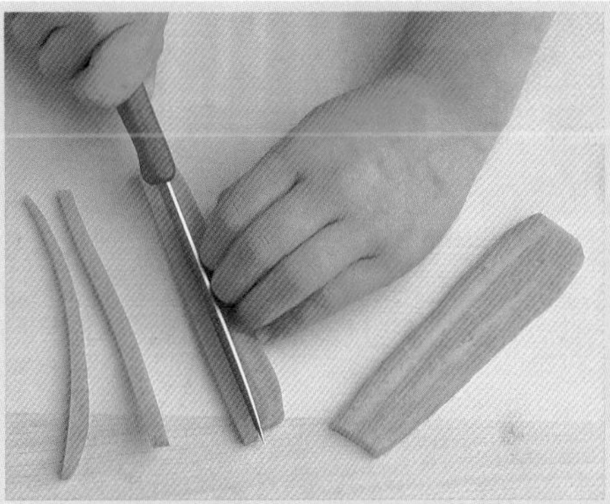

1 Diced means cut into small cubes. To dice a vegetable, cut it in half length-wise, then cut it into thin strips.

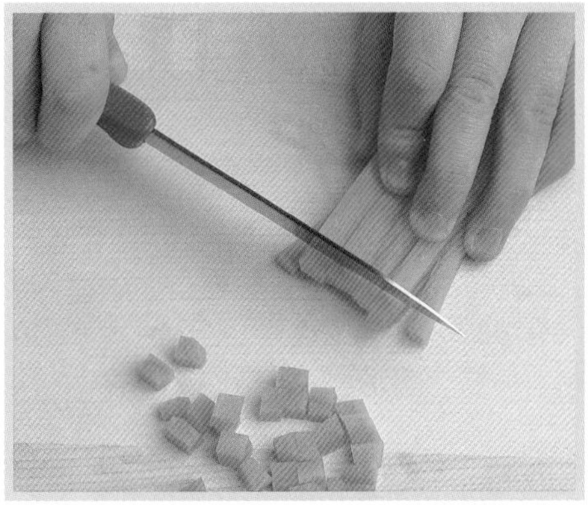

2 Now hold the strips together and slice through them to make small cubes.

Chopping an onion

1 Peel the onion, leaving the root on to hold the onion together.

2 Cut the onion in half and lay one half, cut side down, on the chopping board. Then use a sharp knife to make downward cuts through the onion.

3 Turn the onion and make cuts at right angles across the first cuts, to chop the onion.

Preparing fresh root ginger

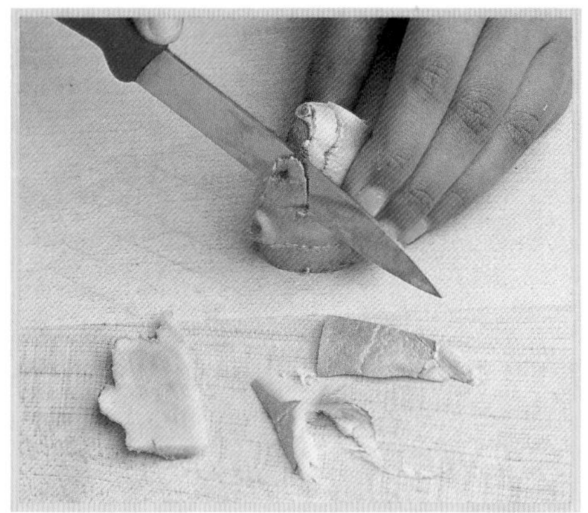

1 Ginger has a woody skin. Use a sharp knife to cut the skin off the piece of root.

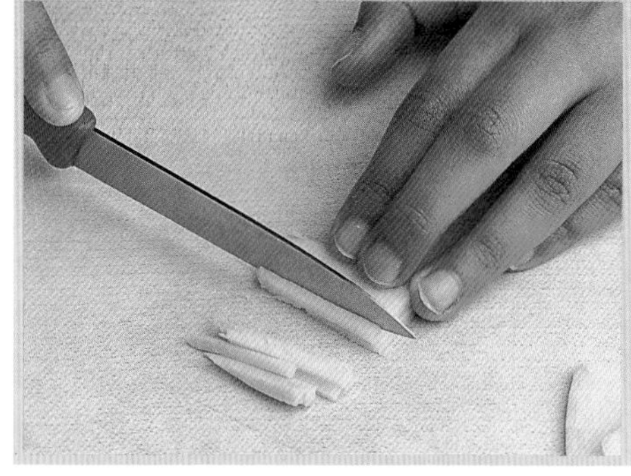

2 Slice the ginger finely. Cut the slices into thin strips, then slice through them to make small cubes.

Peeling and crushing garlic

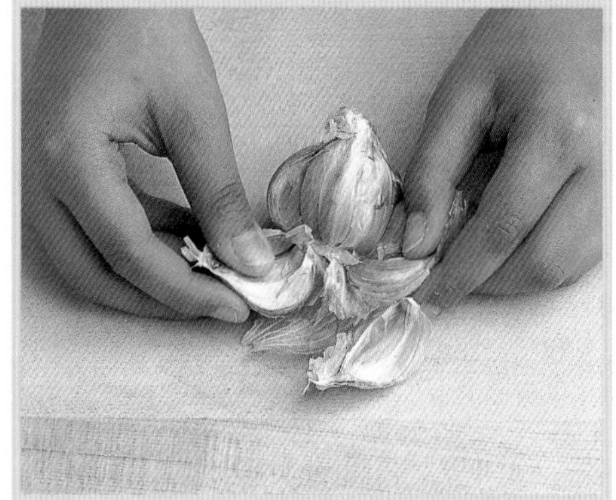

1 Gently pull the garlic cloves away from the bulb of garlic with your fingers.

2 Peel the skin away from the clove of garlic, then put the garlic in a garlic press and close the handle to press the garlic through the holes.

Coring an apple

1 Wash the apple, then push the corer into the apple around the stalk, right down to the base.

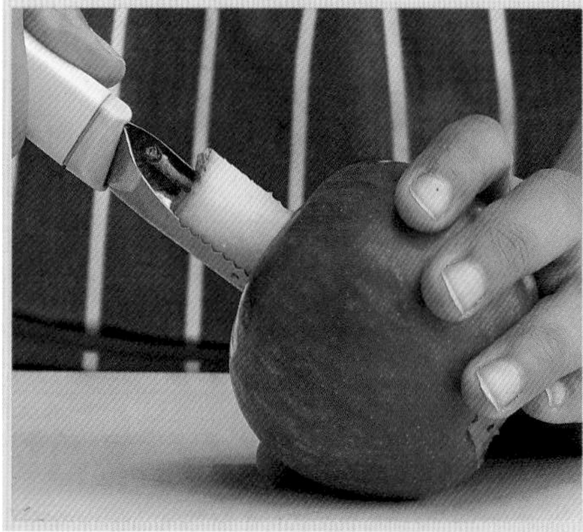

2 Pull the corer out again, to remove a cylinder of apple containing the core and pips.

Grating cheese

Hold the grater down firmly on a chopping board or plate and rub the cheese downwards against the grater, keeping your fingers well away from it.

Stoning fruit

1 Cut the fruit in half with a sharp knife, following the crease down the side of it.

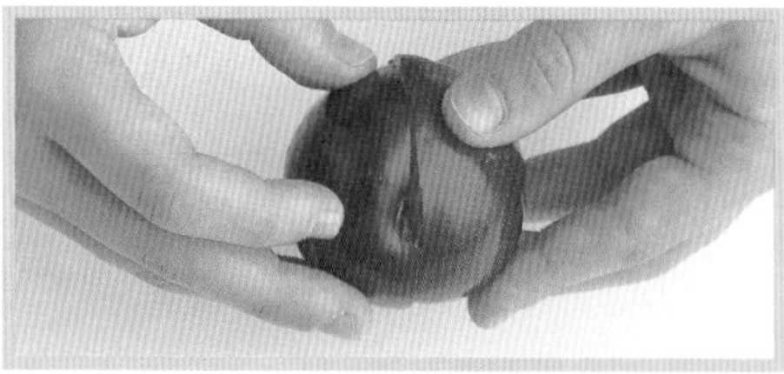

2 Then take the fruit in both hands and twist each half, to loosen it from the stone.

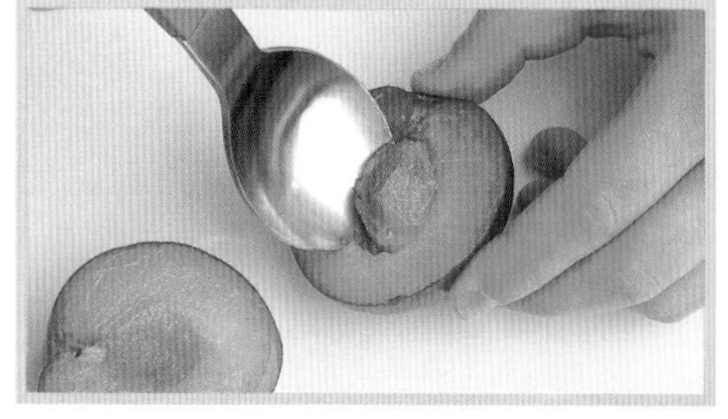

3 Scoop the stone out of the fruit with a spoon.

Dough

This is the word for a thick mixture made mainly of flour, before it has been cooked. It can be cake, bread, biscuit, or pastry dough.

Batter

A flour-based mixture that is runny enough to pour, such as pancake mixture.

Sifting

To sift flour or icing sugar, shake it through a sieve. This gets rid of lumps and makes it light and airy.

Creaming

1 To cream butter and sugar together, cut up the butter and mix it in with the sugar in a bowl using a wooden spoon.

2 Then beat the butter and sugar together as hard as you can with the wooden spoon.

3 The mixture is ready when it is pale and creamy and drops off the spoon easily.

Rubbing in

To do this, rub butter or margarine and flour together with your fingertips until the mixture looks like fine breadcrumbs.

Folding in

This is a gentle way of mixing two things together, to keep them light. Take scoops of the mixture and turn it over and round until it is evenly mixed.

Kneading

To knead dough, fold it and punch it down, then turn it round and keep doing the same thing until the dough is smooth and stretchy.

Beating

To beat something, stir it hard. Beat eggs with a fork or whisk until the yolks and whites are mixed together.

Separating an egg

1 Crack the egg near the middle by tapping it gently against a bowl.

2 Then break the egg open with your thumbs and tip the yolk from one half of the shell to the other, so that the white slips into the bowl below. Put the yolk in a separate bowl.

Whisking

1 To whisk egg whites, beat them quickly and lightly with a whisk.

2 Carry on whisking until the whites are firm and stand up in peaks.

Scoring bread

To score bread, slash the top of the dough with a sharp knife, cutting lines about 1 cm (1/2 in) deep.

Rolling out pastry

1 Sprinkle the table and rolling pin with flour and roll the ball of dough out away from you.

2 Then lift the dough, turn it, and roll it again, sprinkling with more flour if it sticks. Keep doing this until the dough forms the shape you want.

Glazing

Glazing means to coat food with something to make it look glossy. This tart is being brushed with sieved jam.

Seasoning

When you season food, you add salt, pepper, spices, or herbs to it. This gives it extra flavour.

Marinating

To marinate meat, fish, or vegetables, you soak them in a special sauce before cooking them. This adds flavour and makes the food more tender.

Blending

Blending means mixing ingredients together in a blender or food processor. Make sure the lid of the blender is firmly closed.

Grilling

To grill food, you cook it quickly at a high temperature under a grill.

Simmering

Simmering means cooking liquid over a low heat so that it is bubbling gently, but not boiling.

Boiling

Boiling means cooking in water that is boiling (bubbling fiercely).

Frying

To fry food, cook it in hot fat or oil until it is brown and crisp.

Stir-frying

To stir-fry vegetables or meat, put them in a wok or frying pan with a small amount of oil or fat, and cook quickly over a very high heat, stirring all the time.

Baking

To bake is to cook in an oven.

Lining a cake tin

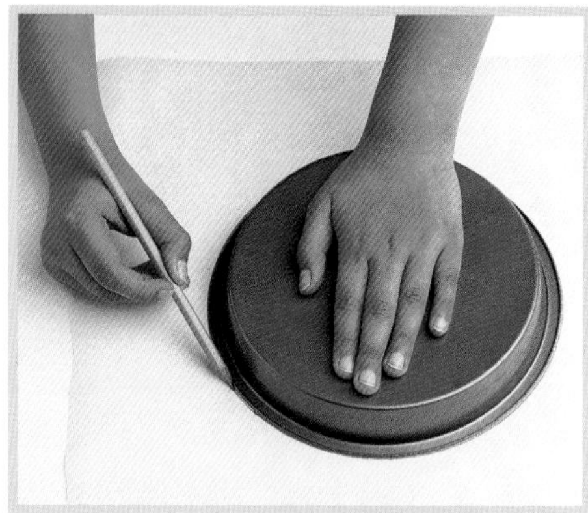

1 Lay the cake tin face down on a sheet of greaseproof paper and draw around it. Then cut out the circle of paper.

2 Brush the inside of the cake tin with melted butter.

3 Then lay the circle of greaseproof paper inside the tin and brush it with more melted butter.

Making an icing bag

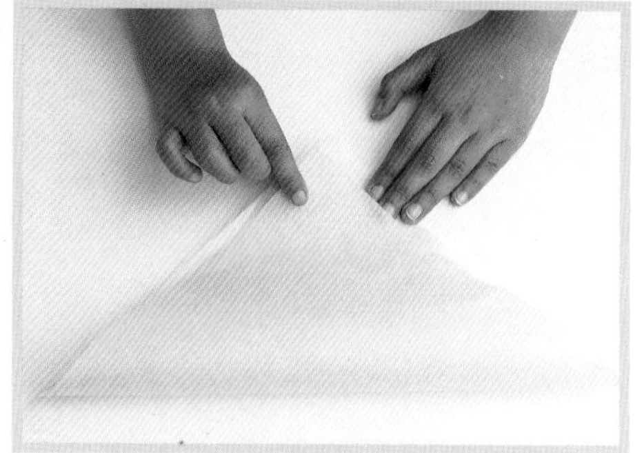

1 Cut out a piece of greaseproof paper 25 cm (10 in) square and fold it in half diagonally.

2 Fold one corner of the folded triangle into the middle point to make a cone.

3 Fold the other corner of the triangle around it so that the three points meet.

4 Then tuck the points inside the cone to hold it firmly in place. Snip the tip off the cone.

Greasing a tin or dish

To grease a baking tin or ovenproof dish, rub it with butter, oil, or lard. This stops food from sticking to it.

Piping icing

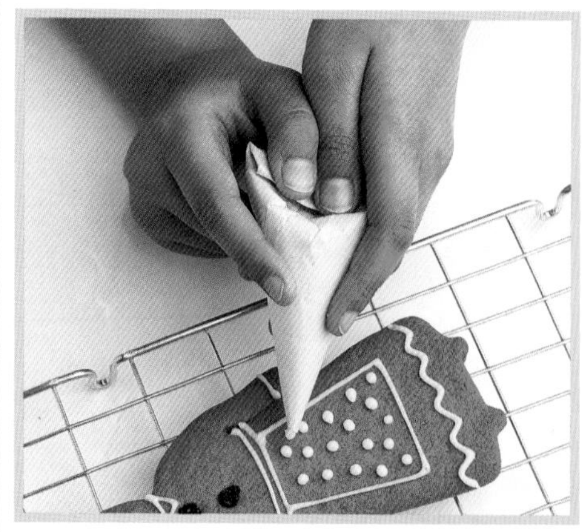

Fill the icing bag with icing. Fold the top of the bag down over the icing and press gently to squeeze out a thin ribbon of icing through the tip of the cone.

INDEX

A

apple
- baked, 106-107
- pie, 110-113
- toast, 34-35

asparagus tarts, 36-39
avocado sandwich filling, 16-17

B

bacon, 65
- burger, 66-67

baked
- eggs, 29
- fruit, 106-107

baking, 125
- bread, 84-85
- pizza, 50-51
- rolls, 86-87

baking powder, 77
banana
- baked, 106-107
- milkshake, 24-25
- split, 99
- tart, 104-105

batter, 114, 123
bean bake, 62-63
beans, 53, 55
beating, 124
beef casserole, 72-73
biscuit cake, 102-103
biscuits
- chocolate chip cookies, 82-83
- gingerbread, 78-79
- icing, 80-81

blending, 125
boiled eggs, 28
boiling, 55, 125
Bolognese sauce, 44-45
bread
- baking, 84-85
- chocolate, 84-85
- herb, 86
- types of, 12-13

broccoli, 54
butter, 77

C

cake decorating, 94-95; *see* also icing
cake tin, lining a, 126
cakes
- biscuit, 102-103
- chocolate sponge, 92-93
- iced sponge, 92-93
- lemon sponge, 92-93
- little sponge, 88-91
- orange sponge, 92-93
- carbonara sauce, 42-43

carrot and cheese sandwich filling, 16-17
carrots, 54
cauliflower, 54
Centigrade, 8
cheese, 26-27
- and carrot sandwich filling, 16-17
- and potato bake, 60-61
- and tomato tarts, 36-39
- creamy sandwich filling, 16-17
- kebabs, 14-15
- fillings for jacket potatoes, 58-59
- on toast, 34-35

cherry sauce for ice-cream, 98-99
chicken, 65
- and ham sandwich filling, 16-17
- kebabs, 68-69
- spicy, 70-71

Chinese fried rice, 48-49
chocolate, 96
- biscuit cake, 102-103
- chip cookies, 82-83
- dipped fruit, 100-101
- icing, 92-93
- loaf, 84-85, 87
- milkshake, 24-25
- sauce for ice-cream, 98-99
- sponge cake, 92-93

chopping
- an onion, 121
- ginger, 122
- herbs, 121

cinnamon toast, 32-33
coconut and cherry cakes, 88-89
cold meats, 13
cooker, using a, 8-9
cookies, chocolate chip, 82-83
coring an apple, 122
courgettes, 55
- and mushroom tarts, 36-39
- pizza, 50-51

cream, 97
creaming, 123
creamy cheese sandwich filling, 16-17
custard, 110, 113

D

decorating
- cakes, 94-95
- pies, 112
- *see* also icing

dicing, 121
dough, 123, 124
- bread/rolls, 84-87
- pastry, 36
- pizza, 50-51

dried fruit, 76

E

egg mayonnaise sandwich
filling, 16-17
eggs, 26
- baked, 29
- boiled, 28
- scrambled, 30-31
- separating, 124
- see also cinnamon toast, French toast

eggy bread *see* French toast

F

Fahrenheit, 8
fats, 77
filling
- for jacket potatoes, 58-59
- for sandwiches/rolls, 16-21

fish, 64
fishermans pie, 74-75
florentines, 100-101
flour, 77
folding in, 123
French toast, 32-33
fruit, 97
- baked, 106-107
- baskets, 108-109
- chocolate-dipped, 100-101
- ice lollies, 22
- kebabs, 14-15
- pie, 110-113
- tarts, 104-105

frying, 125

G

garlic, peeling and crushing, 122
ginger, preparing fresh root, 122
gingerbread, 78-79, 81
glazing, 124
grating, 122
greasing a tin or dish, 126
Greek salad, 56-57
green beans, 55
green salad, 56-57
grilling, 125

H

ham
- and chicken sandwich filling, 16-17
- filling for jacket potatoes, 58-59
- scramble, 30-31
- surprise, 29

hamburgers, 66-67
herb bread, 86
herbs, 52
honey, 76, 77
hot cherry sauce, for ice-cream 98-99

I

ice lollies, 22
ice-cream, sauces for, 98-99
iced sponge cake, 92-93

icing, 80-81, 90-95
  how to make, 80
  how to pipe, 126
icing bag, making a, 126
icing sugar, 76, 77

J
jacket potatoes, 58-59

K
kebabs
  cheese, 14-15
  fruit, 14-15
  meat and vegetables, 68-69
  vegetable, 14-15
kneading, 123

L
lamb kebabs, 68-69
lard, 77
lasagne, 41
lemon sponge cake, 92-93
lining a cake tin, 126

M
margarine, 77
marinating, 68, 125
measuring, 8
meat, types of, 64
meats, cold, 13
menu planner, 116-120
meringue, 108-109
milkshakes, 24-25
mushrooms, 55
  and courgette tarts, 36-39

N
nuts, 96

O
oils, 77
orange sponge cake, 92-93
oven temperatures, 8
oven, using a, 8

P
pancakes, 114-115
party suggestions, 118-119
pasta
  sauces for, 42-45
  types of, 41
pastry, 36-38, 77
  rolling out, 124
peas, 54
picnic suggestions, 116-117
pie, apple, 110-113
piping icing, 126
pitta bread, fillings for, 20-21
pizza
  making, 50-51
  toast, 34-35
popcorn, 23
potatoes, 55
  and cheese bake, 60-61
  jacket, 58-59
  mashed, 75
prawn filling for jacket
  potatoes, 58-59

Q
Quiche Lorraine, 36-39

R
raspberry
  milkshake, 24-25
  sauce for ice-cream, 98-99
rice
  Chinese fried, 48-49
  cooking, 46
  types of, 40
  vegetables and, 46-47
rolling out pastry, 124
rolls
  baking, 84-87
  fillings for, 16-17, 20-21
  types of, 12-13
rubbing in, 123

S
safety rules, 8-9
salad burger, 66-67
salad dressing, 56-57
salad leaves, 52
salads, 56-57
sandwiches, 16-19;
  see also rolls
sauces
  Bolognese, 44-45
  carbonara, 42-43
  chocolate, for ice-cream, 98-99
  hot cherry, for ice-cream, 98-99
  raspberry, for ice-cream, 98-99
  tomato, 44-45
  white, 74
sausage
  kebab, 68-69
  pizza, 50-51
  types of, 13, 65
sautéing, 55
scoring bread, 124
scrambled eggs, 30-31
seasoning, 125
separating an egg, 124
shredding a lettuce, 121
sifting, 123
simmering, 125
slicing, 121
snacks, 12-25
spaghetti, 41, 45
  and carbonara sauce, 42-43
Spanish scramble, 30-31
spices, 64
spicy chicken, 70-71
spinach
  surprise, 29
  tarts, 36-39
steaming, 55
stir-frying, 125
stoning fruit, 122
sugar, 76, 77
sultana cakes, 88-89
sweeteners, 76, 77

T
tagliatelle, 41, 45
tarts
  fruit, 104-105
  savoury, 36-37
temperatures, oven, 8
toast
  apple, 34-35
  cheese on, 34-35
  cinnamon, 32-33
  French, 32-33
tomato
  and Parmesan tarts, 36-39
  sauce for pasta, 44-45
  sauce for pizza, 50-51
  surprise, 29
tools, kitchen, 10-11
tuna
  filling for jacket potatoes, 58-59
  pizza, 50-51
  sandwich filling, 16-17

U
utensils, kitchen, 10-11

V
vegetable fat/oil, 77
vegetables
  cooking, 55
  preparing, 47, 54, 121, 122
  stir-fried with rice, 46-47

W
weighing, 8
whisking, 124
white sauce, 74
white vegetable fat, 77

Y
yeast, 77
yoghurt, 97

Dorling Kindersley would like to thank:
Christopher Gillingwater, Robin Hunter and Rachael Foster for additional design help; Polly Goodman for additional editorial help; Emma Patmore for cooking assistance; and Jonathan Buckley, Polly Arber, Serina Palmer, Selena Singh and Phoebe Thoms for modelling.